CHRISTIANITY RENEWED

(Volume III)

The Return of Christ

D0366298

CHRISTIANITY RENEWED

(Volume III)

The Return of Christ

Maxwell Alexander

PUBLISHING TRUST. INDIA

Copyright © 2007 Marc & Helen Vloeberghs
All rights reserved

No part of this publication may be translated or reproduced in any
form or by any means without the written permission of the copyright
owner. Maxwell Alexander is the pseudonym for the authors Marc and
Helen Vloeberghs.

First edition 1988
Reprints: 1993, 1994, 1995, 1997, 1998, 1999, 2004

Sixth Edition (Revised): February 2008
Reprint: January 2012

ISBN 81–86953–08–6

Cover design and graphics by Armon Rostami

Approved for publication by the National Spiritual Assembly
of the Bahá'ís of India

Bahá'í Publishing Trust
F-3/6, Okhla Industrial Area, Phase-I
New Delhi-110020, India

Printed at: Dora offset, New Delhi-110020

Contents

By the same author

Christianity Renewed:
    Volume I   : The birth of Christianity and other religions
    Volume II : The Hidden Mysteries of the Bible
Soon to be published:
    Volume IV: A visual guide
    VolumeV   : Sharing Christ's Message

Contacting the Authors

If you have any comments or questions, please share them with the authors Marc and Helen Vloeberghs. We have a free newsletter which we send to those who would like to join in an ongoing dialogue. If you would like to email us - it is at mvloeb@gmail.com. We also have a web site which offers 35 free lessons: www.christianityrenewed.com

Acknowledgements

The authors wish to acknowledge with sincere thanks Michael and Yvonne Withiel for their assistance with the review of this revised edition. I would also like to express my gratitude to Armon Rostami (www.rostami.com.au) who provided the new cover design and upgraded the graphics that are used in these three volumes. As Volume three is mainly about prophesies we added in this revised version the chapters "Book of Revelation and 666" and the "Time of the End". These chapters were originally in Volume two.

Dedication

This book is dedicated to our youngest son Alexander who passed away on 4th November, 1996 at 11 years and 11 months old. He has abandoned this mortal life and has flown to the spiritual world.

Foreword

The glorious message of Jesus the Christ has been so completely misunderstood that its survival over the centuries has become one of the greatest proofs of its truth. Nothing but the power of Almighty God could have enabled it to exert the enormous worldwide influence as it has done, and still does.

Christianity today is divided, and unable to stop the decline of humanity into chaos and disaster. Yet its greatest hope, forgotten, unbelieved, or even ridiculed, lies in the very words of Jesus Himself. Several times, the record states, He promised to come again "in the glory of the Father" or as "the Spirit of Truth", and this promise was incorporated in the early centuries into the major official creeds. At various times over the long two thousand years since it was made it became the central theme of Christian hope.

Now, when all the detailed circumstances described in the 24th chapter of St. Matthew, which would attend that wonderful event have come about and are indeed the experience of our daily lives, Christianity is hopelessly divided in itself about Christian truth and its validity, and has ignored the injunction to "watch and pray" for the time when He would come "like a thief in the night".

Maxwell Alexander's excellent presentation of this vital theme rests on the words of Jesus Himself as recorded in the Gospels. He shows how spiritual truths have been taken by simple and naive people to have impossible literal meanings. These have, under the weight of traditional authority, crystallized into doctrines until the Sun of Truth has become clouded over by obscurantism, bigotry, narrow mindedness and prejudice. It is these clouds that disappear with the new sunrise, revealing in all its splendour and beauty the eternal spiritual Truth. This is indeed the renewal, the triumph of Christianity.

David Hofman
(Former member of the Universal House of Justice)

'Abdu'l-Bahá, son of Bahá'u'lláh, who suffered
many years of imprisonment with His Father.

1

Promise of world peace

*"The Great Peace ... for which from age to age the sacred
scriptures of mankind have constantly held the promise,
is now at long last within the reach of the nations. ...
World peace is not only possible but INEVITABLE. It is the
next stage in the evolution of this planet ..."*

— The Universal House of Justice: *The Promise of World Peace*

Is world peace possible?

Social conditions are deteriorating in many countries. The
crumbling of our society is evidenced by the lack of law and order,
corruption, the increase in organized crime, the use of drugs,
a high rate of divorce and the breakdown in family relations.

As we read the newspaper, listen to the radio or watch
the news on television or the internet, we find that millions
of people are suffering due to the chaos caused by global
warming, terrorism, racism, nationalism, injustice, fanaticism,
over population and poverty. We will never forget the tragedy
of the First and Second World Wars, which killed millions of
people. Now we have entered into the 21st century man still
faces the choice of destroying the world or achieving peace
and prosperity.

That such a time of decay would come has been foretold
in the Bible:

*"There will be terrible times in the last days. People
will be lovers of themselves, lovers of money*

...disobedient to their parents... unforgiving, slanderous, without self-control, brutal, not lovers of the good, treacherous, rash, conceited, lovers of pleasure rather than lovers of God.

— 2 Timothy 3:2–5 NIV[1]

We all want peace. Peace begins firstly within ourselves; thereafter we need peace in the family, the community, the nation and eventually peace for the whole world. How can this be achieved?

Promise of world peace

In the Old and New Testaments we find many prophesies that promise a time of peace and justice will come. A time of happiness for all the people in the world!

About 2,500 years ago, Isaiah, a Prophet of the Old Testament, described what God told him, through a vision of the future:

"... the wolf also shall dwell with the lamb ... and the lion shall eat straw like the ox."

— Isaiah 11:7

Does this prophecy which refers to the end of war mean that the wolf which is a natural enemy of sheep will suddenly be a friend? Wolf and sheep, lion and ox are natural enemies. The above quotation can only be understood when we understand the meaning of the different symbols. Wolf, lamb, lion and ox are symbols for different nations that fight against one another. This prophecy holds the promise that a time will come when countries will decide to live in peace side by side as friends.

Coming of the Prince of Peace

Isaiah prophesied that God will send a Messenger, called "the Prince of Peace", whose task is to show mankind the road to world peace.

"For unto us a child is born, and the government shall be upon his shoulder: and his name shall be called ... The Prince of Peace... of the increase of his government and peace there shall be no end."

— Isaiah 9:6–7

Did Jesus have the government on his shoulders?

Jesus made it very clear that the 'government' would not be upon His 'shoulders'. Jesus separated the affairs of God (religious) from those of the Government (secular) by saying:

"Render unto Caesar the things that are Caesar's and unto God the things that are God's."

— Mark 12:27

He further showed that He was not interested in earthly power when He said:

"My kingdom is not of this world."

— John 18:36

Did Jesus claim to be 'the Prince of Peace'?

How could He be the Prince of Peace when He told the people very clearly that He did not come to bring peace. Jesus said:

"Think not that I am come to send peace: I came not to send peace, but a sword."

— Matt. 10:34

Jesus renounced claiming the title of 'Prince of Peace' when He said:

"Suppose ye that I am come to give peace on earth? I tell you, Nay; but rather division:"

— Luke 12:51

The events following the crucifixion of Jesus confirm His words. During the last 2,000 years there have been many religious wars, in which Christians were fighting Christians. These wars fulfilled the above prophecies about Jesus bringing the sword not peace.

World Peace is now possible

The promise of world peace would only be fulfilled at the time of Christ's second coming. That time has now come. God in His infinite wisdom sent Bahá'u'lláh, the Prince of Peace, to fulfil the promise of world peace. In His Tablet to Christendom Bahá'u'lláh explains the high mission of the true Prince of Peace:

> "How tragically has Christendom ignored, and how far it has strayed from, that high mission which He Who is the true Prince of Peace has, in these, the concluding passages of His Tablet to Pope Pius IX, called upon the entire body of Christians to fulfill — passages which establish, for all time, the distinction between the Mission of Bahá'u'lláh in this age and that of Jesus Christ: "Say: O concourse of Christians! We have, on a previous occasion, revealed Ourself unto you, and ye recognized Me not. This is yet another occasion vouchsafed unto you. This is the Day of God; turn ye unto Him.... Verily, He [Jesus] said: 'Come ye after Me, and I will make you to become fishers of men.' In this day, however, We say: 'Come ye after Me, that We may make you to become the quickeners of mankind.'" "Say," He moreover has written, "We, verily, have come for your sakes, and have borne the misfortunes of the world for your salvation. Flee ye the One Who hath sacrificed His life that ye may be quickened? Fear God, O followers of the Spirit [Jesus], and walk not in the footsteps of

every divine that hath gone far astray.... Open the doors of your hearts. He Who is the Spirit [Jesus] verily, standeth before them."

— Shoghi Effendi: *The Promised Day is Come*, p. 105

"O thou who art carried away by the love of God!... Eternal grace is never interrupted, and a fruit of that everlasting grace is universal peace. Rest thou assured that in this era of the spirit, the Kingdom of Peace will raise up its tabernacle on the summits of the world, and the commandments of the Prince of Peace will so dominate the arteries and nerves of every people as to draw into His sheltering shade all the nations on earth. From springs of love and truth and unity will the true Shepherd give His sheep to drink."

— *Selections from the Writings of 'Abdu'l-Bahá*, p. 246

Some Christians think that once the Prince of Peace has come that peace will be automatically established. But the reality is that the remedy given by the Prince of Peace must be applied.

"Should this greatest of all remedies be applied to the sick body of the world, it will assuredly recover from its ills and will remain eternally safe and secure."

— Shoghi Effendi: *The World Order of Bahá'u'lláh*, p. 231

Coming of "the Spirit of Truth"

Jesus said:

"I have yet many things to say unto you, but ye cannot bear them now. Howbeit when He, the Spirit of Truth, is come, He will guide you into all truth: for He shall not speak of himself; but whatsoever He shall hear,

that shall He speak: and He will shew you things to come. He shall glorify me."

— John 16:12–13

This is the age in which Bahá'u'lláh has proclaimed that:

"He, who is the Spirit of Truth is come to guide you unto all truth."

— Bahá'u'lláh: *Tablets of Bahá'u'lláh*, p. 12

Bahá'u'lláh has fulfilled all the criteria for the coming of the Spirit of Truth by His life and Holy Writings. His teachings of the oneness of God, the oneness of religion and of mankind, once put into practice will bring the unity needed so that the Most Great Peace can be established.

Some Christians believe that the Spirit of Truth is the Holy Spirit who according to some of the Gospels came at Pentecost. However a moment's reflection shows us that after Pentecost there was great confusion, division amongst Christians. Although 2,000 years ago Jesus told His disciples to love each other, *"These things, I command you, that you love one another"* (John 15:17), religious leaders have 'in the name of Jesus' created divisions and caused hatred between the different Christian denominations. The disunity of the Christians is a clear sign that the Spirit of Truth didn't come at Pentecost.

'Abdu'l-Bahá explains that the Spirit of Truth is a person not the Holy Spirit:

"He shall not speak of himself; but whatsoever He shall hear, that shall He speak' (John 16:13). It is clear that the Spirit of truth is embodied in a Man Who has individuality, Who has ears to hear and a tongue to speak."

— 'Abdu'l-Bahá: *Some Answered Questions*, p. 109

"The century has dawned when the Spirit of Truth can reveal these verities to mankind, proclaim that very Word, establish the real foundations of Christianity and deliver the nations and peoples from the bondage of forms and imitations... You must listen to the admonitions of this Spirit of Truth. You must follow the example and footprints of Jesus Christ. Read the Gospels. Jesus Christ was mercy itself, was love itself. He even prayed in behalf of His executioners – for those who crucified Him – saying "Father, forgive them: for they know not what they do" If they knew what they were doing, they would not have done it. Consider how kind Jesus Christ was, that even upon the cross He prayed for His oppressors."

— 'Abdu'l-Bahá: *Promulgation of Universal Peace, pp. 41-42*

Coming of 'the Comforter'

Jesus said:

"And I will pray the Father, and He shall give you another Comforter, that he may abide with you for ever."

— John 14:16

Bahá'u'lláh explained that He is the fulfilment of this promise of Jesus. Bahá'u'lláh confirmed the words of Jesus when He proclaimed:

"The Comforter, whose advent all the scriptures have promised, is now come that He may reveal unto you all knowledge and wisdom. Seek Him over the entire surface of the earth, haply ye may find Him."

— Shoghi Effendi: *The World Order of Bahá'u'lláh*, p. 104

The time for One Shepherd and One Fold has come

Jesus promised that during the 'time of the end', He would bring together people from all religions. Jesus taught:

> *"And I have other sheep, that are not of this fold; I must bring them also, and they will hear my voice. So there will be one flock, one shepherd."*

— John 10:16

The 'other sheep' symbolize the members of other religions. We all know there are many religions in this world. They also have their own Holy Books. In each and every Holy Scripture of the world's great religions, there are prophecies about the coming of a great world teacher, a Holy One, an Enlightened One at the time of the end! This great world teacher would establish world unity and world peace; in other words, create one fold and one shepherd, one religion worshiping one God. Shoghi Effendi explains it thus:

> *"The next step in man's evolution – the unification of the human race as one family inhabiting this planet."*

— Compilation of Compilations: Volume II, p. 433

The Return of Christ is an event that is important for the members of all the religions existing in the world for the fulfilment of this great prophecy.

Bahá'u'lláh explains:

> *"Regard men as a flock of sheep that need a shepherd for their protection. This, verily, is the truth, the certain truth."*

— Bahá'u'lláh: *the Kitáb-i-Aqdas*, p. 63

What are the signs of the coming of a new Messenger of God?

In the following chapters we will discuss:

- Does Bahá'u'lláh fulfil the prophecies of the Old and New Testaments, and is He the One that Jesus had foretold would come?

- Will the teachings of Bahá'u'lláh establish unity and world peace?

The Holy Books of all the religions are full of references to the coming of Bahá'u'lláh, and the coming of a new age and the fulfilment of hope for all humankind. However, the significance of these prophecies has been missed because the Scriptures have been interpreted literally. The Bahá'í Faith brings religion once again back to its pure form without any man-made interpretations.

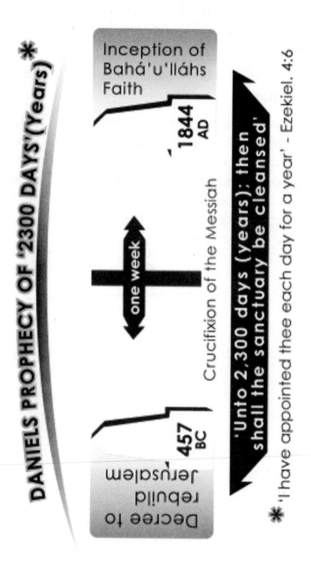

Daniel's prophecy of 2,300 days (years)

"I have appointed thee each day for a year." (Ezek. 4:6)

2

The time of the Second Coming

"He which testifieth those things saith, Surely I come quickly ... Even so, come Lord Jesus."

— Book of Revelation 22:20

When we study the Old Testament we find more than three hundred prophecies relating to the First Advent of Christ as the Messiah. In spite of all this guidance when Jesus came very few people recognized Him. The religious leaders who continuously studied the Old Testament were unable to match His claims with their own literal interpretations of the prophecies. As a result of their spiritual blindness they rejected Jesus as the Messiah and crucified Him.

In the New Testament there are no less than two hundred and fifty separate passages relating to the Second Coming of Christ. Many Christians believe that Jesus is coming back soon. Some church leaders tell them that it is important to remain faithful to Jesus so that when the Lord returns they will be counted among the believers and enter heaven.

About one hundred and fifty years ago, around the year 1844, there was a strong expectation among the Christians that the time of the return of Jesus had finally arrived. This sudden rise in expectation was called the 'Advent movement'. The period was one of the greatest and most dramatic times in Christian history. Many seekers of truth came to the conclusion that Christ would return in the year 1844. This expectation of the return swept across the world and millions of Christians prepared themselves for the 'coming of the Lord'.

The expectation of Christ's return in the 19th century

The expectations that the time of the end was near increased as many strange events occurred between the 1830s and 1840s which people thought fulfilled this prophecy:

> *"And ye shall hear of wars and rumours of wars: see that ye be not troubled: for all these things must come to pass, but the end is not yet. For nation shall rise against nation, and kingdom against kingdom: and there shall be famines, and pestilences, and earthquakes, in divers places."*

— Matt. 24:6-7

History affirms that there were very big earthquakes that destroyed great cities, for example Lisbon in Portugal. Millions of people died from starvation in India and China. Several major wars occurred in Europe and Asia.

There was also an unusually large meteoric shower covering most of North America. This wonderful display of 'falling stars' was followed by the appearance of a brilliant (twin) comet. All these events were seen by thousands of people as signs for the beginning of the end. However, the main reason for the expectation was that hundreds of scholars, independently studying the prophecies in the Bible, came to the overwhelming conclusion that Christ would return in 1844.

Among the Christian leaders in America and Europe who were warning the people to prepare for the return of Christ was William Miller. He studied the Bible for sixteen years and came to the conclusion that Christ would return in 1844.

William Miller even determined that 21 March 1844 was the last day of the prophetic period within which Christ must come. His calculations, based on the prophecies in the Bible, could not be refuted. More than two hundred thousand Christians joined a mass movement called the 'Millerites' and prepared themselves for the 'Advent' or the imminent coming of the Lord.

Another group of Christian members of the German Templar Society even travelled to Palestine in 1868 and set up a colony at the foot of Mount Carmel now part of the city of Haifa. Here they would await the coming of Jesus. At last the great day arrived - but what a disappointment. Nothing spectacular seemed to happen. Church leaders told the disappointed believers that a significant event had occurred in heaven.

A large Christian denomination called the Seventh-day Adventists still believe that Christ started his mission of Judgement in 1844 in heaven based on the writings of their founder Mrs Ellen G. White. One of her most important books is "the Great Controversy" explaining that 1844 is the beginning of the time of the end. Her many visions convinced her fellow Adventists that she possessed the gift of prophecy and she is therefore regarded as a Prophet by the church.

Why did Christians from different parts of the world agree upon the years between 1843 and 1845 as the time for the return of Christ? Because two thousand years ago Jesus promised that He would return to earth when the following three signs occurred:

- The Gospel has been preached throughout the world.
- The time of the Gentiles is fulfilled.

- The prophesies of Daniel, mentioned by Jesus, have been fulfilled.

Indeed, each of these prophesies was fulfilled by the year 1844.

The Gospel preached in all the world

Jesus promised that He would return when the Gospel was being preached throughout the world.
Jesus said:

"And this gospel of the Kingdom will be preached in all the world ... then the end will come."

— Matt. 24:3

British Bible Society considered the fact that the gospel had been taught in all the continents of the world, even in the interior of Africa, as a sign that the first promise was fulfilled and that Christ would soon return.

The time of the Gentiles

Jesus said that He would return when the time of the Gentiles was fulfilled.

"And Jerusalem will be trodden down by the Gentiles, until the times of the Gentiles are fulfilled...and then they shall see the Son of man coming in a cloud with power and great glory."

— Luke 21:24–27

The time of the Gentiles means the time when Jews were not living in Palestine but were living among the Gentiles (non-Jews). About seventy years after the crucifixion of Jesus Palestine was destroyed and the Romans forced the Jews to leave. The Jews continued to live for nearly two thousand years in other countries, not being allowed to return to Palestine. (This period is called the time of the Gentiles). This situation changed suddenly in 1844 when the Jews received permission through the Edict of Toleration to return to Palestine. The Edict of Toleration was the dawn of a new day for the dispersed people of Israel. After centuries of exile and banishment the first seeds of their return were being sown. The time of the Gentiles was fulfilled and soon the Jews started to return to Palestine since Turkey had given them the right to own land. Thus, the year 1844 was indeed the time of the fulfilment of the second sign of Jesus. We could compare 1844 with the time of a conception of a baby which nine months later results in the birth of a baby. In the same way the signing of the Edict in 1844 was the conception or the planting of the seed for the new state which was officially created in 1948.

The time prophesies of Daniel

These prophecies which include the exact time of the Return are very important and are well known. (see diagram on page 10)

Jesus gave this sign to His disciples in direct response to their question: *"When will you return, what are the signs of your coming?"* Jesus asked His disciples to study the following prophecy from the book of Daniel in the Old Testament. Jesus said:

"When ye therefore shall see the abomination of desolation spoken of by Daniel, (whoso read this let him understand) standing in the Holy place."

— Matt. 24:15

Daniel was a prophet who lived in the province of Elam (this country is now called Iran). Daniel described a vision in which one saint speaks to another saint:

*"How long shall be ... the abomination of desolation?
And he said unto me: Unto 2300 days, then shall the
temple be cleansed."*

— Daniel 8:13–14

Daniel's vision of the cleansing of the Jewish Temple in Jerusalem after 2,300 days has great significance for the Jewish people. This temple was the centre for all Jewish religious activities.[2] The "cleansing of the Temple" after 2,300 days has nothing to do with the physical cleaning of a building. It is symbolic language, and refers to the coming of a new Messenger of God who purifies or 'cleans' the religion of God, and removes all man-made ideas and limitations.

The Bible states that the formal written commandment to build the Jewish Temple was issued by the Persian King Artaxerses 457 years before the birth of Jesus (Ezra 7:12). The time from its construction until its cleansing was 2,300 days. Now in Biblical prophecy each day is the equivalent of one calendar year:

"I have appointed thee each day for a year."

— Ezekiel 4:6

"each day for a year"

— Numbers 14:34

Using 457 BC as the starting point, we subtract 456 years from 2,300 years to demonstrate that Daniel's prophecy is fulfilled in the year 1844. Note that from 457 BC (Before Christ) until the beginning of the Gregorian calendar, there are 456 years. (The year 'zero' does not exist, therefore going from 1 BC to AD 1 counts as one year.)

$$456 + 1,844 = 2,300$$

This prophecy is only cited as an example. There are fifteen other prophecies that were fulfilled in the year 1844. A study of all these time prophecies is beyond the scope of this small introduction. What really surprised the scholars was that the time prophecies are not only relating to the Christian calendar but that also the Islamic calendar is pointing to the year 1844! In Islám there is also the expectation for the coming of a great Figure of fulfilment in the year 1230 A.H.! (The year 1230 A.H. is the same as the year 1844 A.D.)

The new Messenger of God will come at the beginning of a new age

That the new Messenger of God will come at the beginning of a new age was prophesied more than two thousand years ago.

Nahum was a minor prophet who lived at a time when people travelled on foot or in chariots pulled by horses. Nahum had a vision of the day of the coming of the new Messenger of God. In those days:

> *"The chariots shall be with flaming torches in the days of His preparation. The chariots shall rage in the streets, they shall jostle one against another in the broad ways: they shall seem like torches, they shall run like the lightnings."*

— Nahum 2:3

How like modern days this sounds, with cars and trucks going 'to and fro' on the highways! Also nowadays people on one side of the world can know immediately what is happening in other parts of the world. Planes travel 'to and fro' to every country of the world.

The year 1844—a new age

The increase of knowledge was prophesied in the Bible as a sign of the new age:

"Many shall run to and fro, and knowledge will be increased."

— Dan 12:4

Before 1844, communications were slow, man travelled by ship, foot or on horseback. From 1844 onwards there was a sudden increase in inventions. The telegraph, radio and telephone which began mass communications as we now know it; the steam engine, automobiles, and airplanes, which began mass transportation; human rights developments such as rights for women and children; all new developments in medicine, technology and sciences — this sudden mysterious increase in inventions was described by many Christian writers in the 19th century as a sign that the new age had started.

1844 was called 'the year of the Great Disappointment'

The Messianic fervour reached its pitch in 1844 but for them nothing happened. Therefore it became known to many Christians as the 'Year of the Great Disappointment'[3] however they were looking in the wrong direction. They expected the Return to occur in the West and they were not aware that the year 1844 was also a time of awakening in the East.

They did not know that many Muslims also quite independently expected the Advent of their Redeemer in that same year of 1844 (1230AH)

They were unaware that it was in Elam, a part of ancient Persia, that Daniel had had his prophetic vision, which, with startling accuracy, foretold the year 1844 as the time of fulfilment.

1844—the year of fulfilment

Although the expectation for the Return of Christ in 1844 is one of the most dramatic periods in the history of Christianity most religious leaders would today prefer to keep it a secret since they are unable to explain why God's word was apparently not fulfilled in 1844. Only if we set aside any prejudices and carefully study world events can we discover that historically there is only one person who proclaimed the beginning of a new age in 1844. His name is the Báb.

Indeed a major religious event did occur in 1844. It was in the East, in Persia, that the Báb proclaimed that He had brought a Message from God. This event happened on 23 May 1844 at a time when the expectation for the Return of Christ had reached its highest pitch in the West.

On that very same day in the West, Samuel Morse, the inventor of the telegraph, sent the first official telegraphic message from Washington to Baltimore. He used a text from the Bible: *"What hath God wrought."* This great invention heralded in the new age of telecommunications signalling man's ability to communicate worldwide.

The Báb called 1844 as the beginning of the fulfilment of all the Holy Scriptures. He said:

> *"Awake, awake, for lo! the Gate of God is open, and the morning Light is shedding its radiance upon all mankind."*
>
> — The Báb: *The Dawn Breakers*, p. 85

The name Báb translated into English means 'the gate' or 'the door'. The Báb proclaimed that he was the 'door' through which would come the One promised in all the Holy Books, Who would establish the one fold of God. As Jesus said:

> *"But he that entereth in by the door is the shepherd of the sheep."*
>
> — John 10:2

Since the Báb is the only person who made such a mighty announcement in 1844, all Christians should study His life to investigate if He is indeed a Messenger from God.

Similarities between the Báb and Jesus

Anyone who studies the amazing life of the Báb will quickly see many similarities with that of the life of Jesus. They were both youthful, both known for their meekness and loving kindness. Both of them challenged the laws and rites of the religion in which they were born. Their chief enemies were the religious leaders of the land. The period of their ministry was very brief. They were both forcibly brought before the government authorities and subjected to a public interrogation. Both were scourged and paraded through the streets following this interrogation. They were both martyred in a cruel and inhumane fashion thereby sacrificing Their lives for humanity. Confusion, bewilderment and despair seized their followers in each case following their martyrdom.

It is well documented how many Christians were killed by the Romans for their belief in Jesus. In a similar way, the Persian government and the Muslim clergy would try to destroy the new religion brought by the Báb. More than twenty thousand followers of the Báb were tortured and killed in public. Some of them were crucified; others flayed, burned, impaled, shod like horses or tied to the muzzles of heavy guns. It is recorded that they gave their lives for the Báb as martyrs, since they preferred to be killed rather than to deny the Báb. Are such acts of courage not worthy of investigation?

Is this not similar to the Christian martyrs who were brutally killed by the Romans for their belief in Jesus?

The Báb prepares the way

The terrible persecution of the followers of the Báb was reported in local newspapers yet Christianity remained unaware for many years of this tremendous event that started in 1844 in faraway Persia. They only had a very limited vision of what the return of Christ really meant. Just as John the Baptist had prepared the way for the coming of Jesus about two thousand years ago, the Báb prepared the way for the coming of the great Redeemer of mankind. The time for one Shepherd and one fold had finally arrived. Christians, Hindus, Buddhists and Muslims can now find a common home under one roof. Not only in the Bible but also prophecies appear in all the Holy Books that pinpoint 1844 as the year of renewal. The Báb said this to His followers:

> *"You are the witnesses of the Dawn of the promised Day of God. ... Ponder the words of Jesus addressed to his disciples, as He sent them forth ... Arise in His name, put your trust wholly in Him, and be assured of ultimate victory"*
>
> — The Báb: *The Dawn Breakers*, pp. 92–3

3

Christ's descent upon the clouds of heaven

*"Judge fairly; Were the prophesies recorded in the
Gospel to be literally fulfilled; were Jesus, Son of
Mary accompanied by angels, to descend from the
visible heaven upon the clouds; who would dare to
disbelieve, who would dare to reject the truth?"*

— Bahá'u'lláh: *The Book of Certitude*, p. 81

In 1844, many Christians were looking to the sky expecting
Jesus to come down out of the visible sky, standing on a cloud,
and surrounded by angels blowing on trumpets. Some
Christians even built churches without roofs so that they
would be able to watch the sky continuously and not miss
this spectacular event!

Other Christians donned new white clothes in preparation
for Jesus to carry them straight to Heaven. However, nothing
happened! Why, they asked, did Jesus, who clearly promised
that He would return in 1844, not come back on a cloud from
Heaven in a literal sense as they expected? The reason is
that many of the signs given in the Bible have a spiritual
meaning. Only when looked at with spiritual eyes is the truth
understandable.

Jesus came down from Heaven

Two thousand years ago the Jews were expecting the coming
of the Messiah, which is a Hebrew word that means 'the
anointed one' or 'king'.[4]

Why did they not accept that Jesus was indeed their promised Messiah or the Christ (Greek for Messiah). The religious leaders rejected the 'King' because, in their opinion, Jesus did not fulfil the prophecies in the Old Testament in a literal sense. The Jews were strong believers in Moses and they knew the Old Testament very well. They knew the signs for the coming of the Christ. They expected the Messiah to come seated on a throne as a King surrounded by angels! *"Upon the throne of David, and upon his kingdom...Lord of hosts will perform this"* (Isaiah, 9:7) Misunderstanding this prophecy the religious Jewish leaders told the people that Jesus was a false prophet as He was not a king and there were no angels to be seen.

Also in the Old Testament, Daniel had a vision of *"one like the Son of Man"* coming in *"the clouds of heaven"* (Dan.7:13)

Therefore, the Jews expected the Messiah to come with the clouds of heaven.

They were shocked when Jesus, who always called Himself 'the Son of Man', confirmed that He had already fulfilled this prophecy when He said: *"For I came down from Heaven."* (John 6:38) Naturally, the Jews mocked him and said:

"Is this not Jesus, the son of Joseph, whose father and mother we know? How does he now say, I have come down from heaven?"

— John 6:42

The Jews had 'eyes but they did not see'. They knew where Jesus was born and could not accept that He meant that His spirit had come from heaven not his body.

Signs for His Second Coming are the same as for the First

Christians have to be extremely careful, because they often, like the Jews of the past, interpret the Bible in a literal and material sense. This is especially true as the signs for the Second Coming are similar to the signs for the First Coming. Since Jesus has already given us a spiritual explanation of how those signs were fulfilled through Him, it is logical that we should use the same spiritual meanings for the Return of Christ! Therefore, it is the spirit of Christ (not the physical body of Jesus) that would symbolically descend from heaven, 'to dwell among us' as 'the Word made Flesh', but His body would be that of a human being!

Jesus used symbols from nature when He spoke about the signs for His Return:

> *"Immediately after the oppression of those days shall the sun be darkened and the moon shall not give her light and the stars shall fall from heaven."*

— Matt. 24:29

Let us look at this verse in more detail:

"Immediately after the oppression"
Bahá'u'lláh wrote:

> *What 'oppression' is more grievous for the soul seeking the truth and wishes to attain unto the knowledge of God should not know where to go for it and from whom to seek it?*

— Bahá'u'lláh: *The Kitáb-i-Íqán, The Book of Certitude*, p. 31

Paul explains in 2 Tim. 3:1 *that "in the last days perilous times will come"* and people will be *"always learning and never able to come to the knowledge of Truth."* This is definitely the case in our time – the oppression of understanding. If somebody is seeking for truth which church can he turn to as they are divided into many denominations? Which Christian leader could that seeker trust? Christian leaders have different opinions about moral issues such as divorce and birth control to mention just a few. Politics and different interpretations are confusing Christians. The same is true in all the other religions. In fact the 'oppression'[5] of the Truth of the previous Revelation is always evident at the time of every new Revelation.

Some Bibles use the term 'tribulation' instead of its actual Greek meaning 'oppression'. Both mean the same: a time of spiritual confusion and destruction. The most important is the 'spiritual confusion' as it is a greater calamity for the eternal soul to be lost by confusion than for temporary bodies to be destroyed.

Bahá'u'lláh explained the biblical use of the word 'oppression':

> *"As to the words—'Immediately after the oppression of those days'—they refer to the time when men shall become oppressed and afflicted, ... when certain knowledge will have given way to idle fancy, and corruption will have usurped the station of righteousness ..." "This 'oppression' is the essential feature of every Revelation. Unless it cometh to pass, the Sun of Truth [Manifestation of God] will not be made manifest."*

> — Bahá'u'lláh: *The Book of Certitude*, p. 31

Only after these 'perilous times' when truth is usurped by corruption does the 'Sun of Truth' dawn over the horizon. By 'oppression' is meant a time when people seek spiritual truth but they do not know where to find true guidance. In such times of spiritual confusion people turn to the false gods of nationalism, racism, communism, materialism and capitalism—which cause wars confusion and destruction.

"The sun shall be darkened"
When the sunlight is veiled no light reaches our planet and

its surface is darkened. In the Bible, the sun is often used as a symbol for God. *"For the Lord God is a sun ...."* (Psalms 84:11). In other places, the sun is a symbol for the Messenger of God. Malachi defines the 'day of the Lord' as the day when *"the Sun of righteousness [shall] arise with healing in his wings ...."* (Mal. 4:5–2)

The sun mentioned in this prophecy is therefore not the sun that is visible to our physical eyes. It is a spiritual sun. Just as the sun in the sky gives us light and warmth, the spiritual sun gives us knowledge and guidance. The Divine teachers, for example Moses and Jesus, give us spiritual light (knowledge) and are called 'the Spiritual Suns of Truth'.

"These Suns of Truth are the universal Manifestations of God in the worlds of His attributes and names"

— Bahá'u'lláh: *Book of Certitude*, p. 33

Today due to the misunderstandings of man-made interpretations the truth is veiled and many people are turning away from the original message of Jesus. Only a few have recognized the new sunrise with the coming of Bahá'u'lláh.

"the moon shall not give her light"

The moon gives us light at night. The religious leaders are like the moon which has no light of its own but reflects the light of the sun. Because they are darkened in their views they are unable to faithfully reflect the light of their Prophet (or spiritual sun) we are now living in a spiritual night. Thus these religious leaders and their teachings have lost their influence. They no longer offer guidance to mankind.

"The stars fall from heaven"

Any student of science will tell you that a star is a thousand times bigger than this small earth and therefore it is impossible for a star to fall from heaven onto this planet. The effect would be similar to that of thousands of mountains falling on a small rock. If one star was to fall on this earth, the earth would be utterly destroyed.

The stars guide us at night. People all around the world use stars to help them find their way on the land and on the sea. In the same way, people look for spiritual guidance from religious leaders and priests. These religious leaders are often called 'the stars' in the Bible:

"... they that turn many to righteousness as the stars ..."

— Dan 12:3

Jesus warns us not to ask religious leaders for advice: He tells us:

"Let them alone: they be blind leaders of the blind. And if the blind lead the blind, both shall fall into the ditch."

— Matt. 15:14

Jesus rebukes the religious leaders who rejected Him in the strongest terms. He called them 'blind leaders', 'hypocrites', 'graves' and 'serpents'.[6]

"Ye hypocrites ... This people draweth nigh unto me with their mouth, and honoureth me with their lips; but their heart is far from me. But in vain they do worship me, teaching for doctrines the commandments of men."

— Matt. 15:7

The same is true during the time of the Return. Bahá'u'lláh says of these religious leaders:

"On their tongue the mention of God hath become an empty name; in their midst His Holy Word a dead letter."

— Bahá'u'lláh: *The Book of Certitude*, p. 9

Therefore, 'fall of the stars' symbolizes the fall of religious leaders because they do not follow the true teachings of God anymore, but rather they follow their own ideas and imaginations. Hence, the religious leaders will be incapable of guiding their congregations at the time of Christ's Return. Jesus hinted to this when He said:

"When the Son of man cometh, shall he find faith on the earth?

— Luke 18:8

More signs

Jesus continued answering the questions of His disciples:

"And then shall appear the sign of the Son of man in Heaven; and then shall all the tribes of the earth mourn, and they shall see the Son of man coming in the clouds of heaven with power and great glory: And he shall send his angels with a great sound of a trumpet ..."

— Matt. 24:29–31

"and then shall appear the sign of the son of man"
The signs are the forerunners who prepare the heart of the people for the coming of the new Messenger. John the Baptist announced the coming of the Messiah. In the Bahá'í Faith it was the Herald, the Báb, who in 1844 announced the coming of Bahá'u'lláh. The sign can also be understood as the appearance of a star at the time of His Coming. There is the biblical story of the star of Bethlehem (Matt. 2:2) which led the three "wise men from the East" to the infant Jesus. In a like manner the great twin comet that appeared in the sky in 1843 increased the expectation among the Christians that the Return of Christ was near.

"And then shall the tribes of earth mourn"

"The people will "lament the loss of the previous [spiritual] Sun of divine beauty, of the Moon of knowledge, and of the Stars of divine wisdom."

— Bahá'u'lláh: *Book of Certitude*, p. 66

"They shall see the Son of man"
The Promised One shall descend from the heaven of the Will of God in the form of a human.

"in the clouds of heaven"
A well known sign for the Return of Christ is that He will appear in a cloud. This cloud has a profound spiritual meaning.

What is a cloud?
Science teaches us that a cloud is a visible mass of tiny, condensed water droplets or ice crystals suspended in the atmosphere. Water evaporates from the surface of the earth, water surfaces (rivers and the sea), and is transpired from the surfaces of plant leaves. Some of this water vapour rises into the atmosphere to form clouds in the sky. You cannot ride a cloud. If you tried, you would fall straight through it. Airplanes fly straight through clouds.

Did Jesus really want us to believe that He will come back riding on a cloud around the entire planet for all to see Him? The 'clouds of heaven' have a different meaning—a spiritual meaning. For example, imagine yourself in a village in the mountains. In the morning when you get up, the clouds are close to the ground and it is difficult to see the mountain tops around you. Clouds obscure your view. This is the intended meaning of clouds in the Old Testament. They symbolize limits to our vision that makes it difficult for us to understand something when God speaks to us.

During His First Coming, Jesus came in the clouds of heaven!

The body of Jesus came from the womb of Mary, but His Christ spirit came from heaven. Jesus said:

> *"And no man hath ascended up to heaven, but he that came down from heaven, even the Son of man which is in heaven."*

(John 3:13)

In this verse, Jesus clearly confirms that His spirit is in heaven. For Jesus, heaven is not the physical sky or space above us.

When Jesus said *'I am coming in the clouds'* it meant that at His Return it will be difficult for us to recognize Him. The clouds are all the hindrances or barriers that prevent us from seeing Him as a spiritual being, because He had all the normal human physical limitations.[7]

These were the same 'clouds' in which Jesus came the first time. Although the Jews could see Jesus standing in front of them, they were still unable to believe in Him as their spiritual eyes were closed. Jesus often spoke about people who have eyes but do not see. Only those people whose spiritual eyes are open will be able to see Him!

It will be difficult to recognize Him at His Second Coming

When Jesus said *'I am coming in a cloud'*, it meant that it will be difficult to spiritually recognize Him when He returns. Superstitions will cloud or veil our eyes. The cloud is all the hindrances and barriers to recognizing Him as a human being, born of an earthly mother. History will repeat itself. As with the First Advent, religious leaders will oppose Him. He will again be called 'a false prophet'. The spiritual eyes of the majority of people will be closed and it will take a long time for people to recognize Him.[8] Bahá'u'lláh clearly claims that He came from heaven when He wrote:

"He verily, hath come down from heaven, even as He came down from it the first time. Beware lest ye dispute that which He proclaimeth, even as the people before you disputed His utterances.

— *Tablets of Bahá'u'lláh*, p. 11

"And he shall send his angels with a great sound of a trumpet"

Who are the angels? Angels are symbolic of the servants of the true God. Another terminology for the word 'angel' is saint, for example in the verse:

"At the coming of our Lord Jesus Christ with all his saints"

— 1 Thessalonians 3:13

The saintly disciples of Jesus, who spread His message through suffering and martyrdom, were the angels. Likewise, the followers of the Báb and Bahá'u'lláh who displayed the greatest courage and heroism in the face of fierce opposition were also angels. Despite the fact that more than twenty thousand followers were tortured and killed during the early days of the Faith they continued to proclaim the message of His coming with angelic fortitude.

"With the great sound of a Trumpet"

The Old Testament records a number of occasions when God used a person as a 'trumpet' to warn the people. For example, Ezekiel was appointed by God as a watchman or he 'who blows the trumpet'.

"But if the watchman see the sword come, and blow not the trumpet, and the people be not warned ... So

thou, O son of man [Ezekiel], I have set thee a watchman unto the house of Israel ..."

— Ezekiel 33:6–7

Also Joel says:

"Blow the trumpet in Zion."

— Joel 2:1

Zion is another name for Palestine, now Israel. As we will later see, Bahá'u'lláh blew the trumpet of His teachings from Palestine. His teachings went from a dark prison to the four corners of the earth.[9]

Christ will come back as a 'thief in the night'

Most Christians believe that the Return of Christ will be a great event in which Christ will return surrounded by angels with a great sound of trumpets in which all eyes will see him. But in the same chapter, Jesus also warned the disciples that He will return as *"a thief in the night"*. (Matt. 24:43)

What did Jesus really mean? This statement seems to contradict the previous ones. A thief does not come during the day so that "all eyes can see him", with "angels with a great sound of trumpets" and "riding in the clouds". A thief does not come with the sound of trumpets. A thief comes quietly and unexpectedly. Hence, you may wake up in the morning to find all your possessions have been stolen. However, you did not notice the thief come into your house because you were fast asleep!

If we expect the Return to be a spectacular display of trumpets sounding, stars falling out of heaven, the darkening of the sun and moon, and angels appearing; then we are making the same mistakes that the Jews made two thousand years ago![10]

The Return of Christ is not a theatrical event that will be immediately clear and evident to everyone. To protect humankind from destroying itself, a new Messenger of God comes to let His light of truth shine in the spiritual darkness. Bahá'u'lláh, who is the Messenger of God for this age, came unexpectedly and unknown. He was banished and imprisoned. Only those people "who have ears and can hear" and those "who have eyes and can see" were able to recognize Him as the Promised One of all religions.

4

Spiritual meaning of Return

"Know that the return of Christ for a second time doth not mean what the people believe, but, rather, signifieth the One promised to come after Him. He shall come with the Kingdom of God and His power (or reign) is in the world of hearts and spirits and not in that of matter."

— Compilations, *Bahá'í Scriptures*, p. 477

Return of the Spirit not the body

Some people think that the Return of Christ means that they shall see in bodily form the identical person of Jesus of Nazareth who walked the streets of Jerusalem two thousand years ago. When Jesus referred to John the Baptist as the return of Elijah He was helping the His disciples to understand the hidden or spiritual meaning of Return. It is the return of the spirit not of the body which is important.

It helps to understand Jewish thinking at the time of Jesus. Most Jews of that time knew the Old Testament very well. The prophet Elijah was well-known among the Jews since the story of his life is recorded in the Old Testament. He was supposed to have performed many miracles. It is said that at the end of his life he did not die but instead went up in a chariot to Heaven:

"and there appeared a chariot of fire, and horses of fire ... and Elijah went up ... into heaven."

— 2 Kings 2:11

The Jews knew from their Scriptures that before the Messiah came Elijah would return:

"Behold, I will send you Elijah the prophet before the coming of the great and dreadful day of the Lord."

— Malachi 4:5–6

With this in mind many Jews were waiting for Elijah to return as a sign for the Coming of the Messiah. Since they interpreted the prophecy in a literal physical sense they believed that the same Elijah would descend physically from the visible sky!

As this strange event did not happen the Jewish priests used it to disprove Jesus' claim that He was the Messiah because, in their eyes, one of the signs announcing the coming of the Messiah remained unfulfilled! The disciples of Jesus were also confused, and they asked Jesus for an explanation of why Elijah had not returned.

"And Jesus answered and said unto them, Elijah truly shall first come, and restore all things. But I say unto you, that Elijah is come already and they knew him not, but have done unto him whatsoever they liked. Then the disciples understood that he spake unto them of John the Baptist."

— Matt. 17:11

Jesus explains in the above text that the prophecy that said 'Elijah must come first' was actually fulfilled, not with the return of the person and body of the former Elijah, rather Elijah had returned 'in the spirit and power' in the person of John the Baptist.

Luke also recorded the fulfilment of this prophecy when he wrote about the birth of John the Baptist;

"he shall go before him in the spirit and power of Elijah ..."

— Luke 1:17

John the Baptist had a different identity from that of Elijah who lived two hundred years earlier. The spirit of John the Baptist was the same as the spirit of Elijah. Indeed, the prophetic and spiritual attributes of Elijah were again manifested in John the Baptist.

Similar to Jewish expectations about Elijah, many Christians believe that the same physical Jesus will return. The Return of Christ is not the return of the same individual as Jesus of Nazareth who lived on this earth two thousand years ago. The Return of Christ is the Return of the Christ spirit, and the reappearance of the spirit and power of Jesus in the person of a different man with a new name and a new identity.

'Christ' is not the name of a person but a title. The word Christ is a Greek word that is derived from the Hebrew 'Messiah'. As the Gospels were written in Greek, both the Hebrew and the Greek title are often used together. For example:

"The woman saith unto him, I know that Messiah cometh, which is called Christ ..."

— John 4:25

Christ means, the 'anointed One', or as most Christians call him, 'the Saviour'. Since it is a title, it is of course possible for several people to have the same title.

The return of Christ is the reappearance of the 'Saviour'. It is the return of the spirit and power of Christ in the person of a different Messenger of God.

Examples from nature

In the Bahá'í Writings, we find simple explanations from nature about the idea of the return. It really means the return of those qualities that previously existed.

'Abdu'l-Bahá, the son of Bahá'u'lláh explained:

"For example, there was a flower last year, and this year there is also a flower; I say the flower of last year has returned. Now, I do not mean that same flower in its exact individuality has come back; but as this flower has the same qualities as that of last year—as it has the same perfume, delicacy, colour and form—I say, the flower of last year has returned, and this flower is the former flower."

— Tablets of 'Abdu'l-Bahá, vol. I, p. 138

If we speak about the return of Christ then we are thinking of another Divine Teacher with a new name who has the same spiritual qualities as Jesus. The qualities of Jesus that attracted the sincere seekers in the time of Jesus were His goodness, knowledge, love, understanding, compassion, power, and justice, to name but a few. Those qualities are the qualities of God. In a similar way only those people who really love God will be able to recognize the same divine qualities in Bahá'u'lláh and the other Messengers of God.

Jesus returned with power and great glory

Jesus confirmed that He had already fulfilled the signs that He came with power and glory when he said: *"All power is given unto me in heaven and on earth"* (Matt. 28:18). Jesus prayed to the Father and thanked God for giving him *"power over all flesh"* (John 17:1–2) Yet to those who were there at the time and witnessed His humiliation at the hands of His enemies He had no earthly power. This was also prophesised in the old Testament *"He is despised and rejected of men: a man of sorrows, and acquainted with grief: and we hid as it were our faces from him: he was despised, and we esteemed him not"* (Isaiah 53:3) His power was spiritual not physical. His glory is shown in the triumph he had over his enemies spiritually – they crucified Him but His cause lives on.

> *"For well nigh two thousand years this sovereignty of Christ hath been established, and until now it endureth, and to all eternity that Holy Being will be exalted upon an everlasting throne."*

> — *Selections from the Writings of 'Abdu'l-Bahá*, p. 45-6

To help us understand the difference between earthly and heavenly power Jesus confirms that He is a spiritual King who has spiritual power seated on the throne of David, but His Kingdom is not of this world. This was also prophesised in the Old Testament:

> *"And there was given him dominion, and glory, and a kingdom, that all people, nations, and languages, should serve him: his dominion is everlasting dominion, which shall not pass away, and his kingdom that which shall not be destroyed"*

> — Daniel, 7: 14

Spiritual Signs not physical

John the Baptist confirms in Luke 3:5 that Jesus fulfilled the 'strange' prophecy in Isaiah 40:4 that with the coming of the Messiah: *"Every valley shall be exalted, and every mountain and hill shall be made low"*. Of course, this prophecy was definitely not fulfilled in a literal way as every visitor to Israel can see that it is still full of mountains and valleys exactly as it was in the days of Jesus.

The Jews of Jesus' time rejected Him because the promised signs were not fulfilled in a literal physical manner. However, Jesus confirmed He was the Messiah and that he had already fulfilled the prophecies in a symbolic way.

Jesus exclaimed:

"Why is my language not clear to you? Because you are unable to hear what I say."

— John 8:43 NIV

5

Book of Revelation and 666

"Blessed are the just souls, who seek the truth."

— 'Abdu'l-Bahá: *Some Answered Questions*, p. 82

The Book of Revelation is difficult to understand. It is full of symbols and analogies. During the last two thousand years, these symbols have been interpreted in many different ways and have been the cause of division in the Christian churches.

Let us now look at some of the subjects dealt with in the Book of Revelation. Sometimes the visions are joyful, telling us about the coming of the next Messenger of God after Jesus. In other parts of the book, visions are of dreadful beasts such as the one popularly known as "666", which is "the number of the beast".

The beast with the number 666

This is a minor subject in the Book of Revelation, but in certain countries missionaries often preach in villages about the number '666' and they attach great importance to it. Many people are especially fascinated with the number '666' when they hear some of the fanciful interpretations made of it. Hence, they often regard it as the greatest evil that can come into their life. This is not true!

The story of the number 666 is a very good example of how things can be taken out of context, exaggerated beyond proportion, and unfortunately cause division between Christian churches, who often accuse each other of being the '666'. As soon as one church group accuses another of being the beast with the number 666, love and unity disappear, and hatred and division take their place.

The Bahá'í Writings offer a lot of guidance for a better understanding of the true meaning of the number 666. Where does this term '666' come from? Jesus never mentioned it. In fact, it is only mentioned once in the Book of Revelation. Let us now look at the only reference given in the Bible regarding the number 666. (If it really was important, then we would expect Jesus to have also mentioned it!)

"Here is wisdom. Let him that has understanding count the number of the beast: for it is the number of a man, and his number is 666."

— Revelation 13:18

Many Christians are worried about the number 666, as they believe this beast is coming soon. However, this also is not true. The text tells us that the beast is a man and that 666 is his number. To understand the meaning of the number 666, it is important to know the history of mankind, especially any significant religious events that occurred in the year 666. In Arabia, in the year AD 666, Mu'áwiyyah, the leader of a powerful tribe called the Umayyad, strongly opposed the teachings of the religion of God. He engaged in blasphemous forgery that divided the believers. In his attempt to take over power and use the religion of God for his own purpose, he attacked the holy cities of Islam, which were the birth place and the burial place of Muhammad, the Messenger of God. The "beast" is the symbol for the leader of the Umayyad. His number is 666 because of the year 666 during which he carried out his evil plan to destroy God's religion.

John gives a description of the beast, *"and behold a great red dragon, having seven heads and ten horns"* (Revelation 12:3). The seven heads and ten horns have a special meaning. It is a symbol for the Umayyad tribe who misguided the followers of Muhammad. The seven heads symbolize the seven countries over which the Umayyad ruled, and the ten horns are the names of the ten leaders of the Umayyad tribe.

4 BC	33	570	622 632	666
Birth of Jesus	AD 26	Birth of Muhammad	Death of Muhammad	Mu'áwiyah destroys the spirit of Islam

Meaning of the number 666

The time of the 666 was a long time ago. Therefore, Christians belonging to denominations that place great importance on "666" do not have to worry any more as it has already happened.

Book of Revelation a spiritual vision of the future

John had a great vision that the Revelation of God was not completed by Jesus, but that it will continue into the future.

To understand the Book of Revelation better, it is important to know that nearly six hundred years after the death of Jesus a new religion called Islam was born. Islam is today one of the largest religions of the world, with more than seven hundred million believers. When John had his visions about the future, he saw the birth of this new revelation of God and described it in a symbolic language. Many Bible scholars tried to explain the Book of Revelation without taking into account the world-shaking historical events that occurred around the year AD 622 with the rise of Islam. Additionally, many of the explanations of the events in the Book of Revelation given by Bible scholars are in contradiction to science. They do not recognize that the language used is symbolic, not literal. Bahá'ís believe that religion must not disagree with science.[1] The Bahá'í writings also tell us that a study of Islam, as one of the major influences which shaped the destiny of mankind, is essential to gain a logical understanding of the Book of Revelation.

The coming of Muhammad

To understand better the role that Islam plays in the plan of God for humanity, we must learn more about the life of Muhammad, the founder of Islam. Muhammad was a great divine Educator.

Muhammad was born around the year AD 570 in Arabia, a big desert country in the Middle East. At that time, the Arabian tribes were in the lowest depths of savagery and barbarism. These tribes kept plundering and destroying each others property.

Among these fierce, blood-thirsty people, Muhammad arose as a great Educator from God. The people worshipped many idols, but Muhammad, like Abraham, taught them to believe in only the one true God. Muhammad, who had never been taught to read or write, revealed a book called the Qur'án, which is the 'Bible' of the Muslims. It was considered a great miracle that God chose a supposedly illiterate person to produce a book of divine teachings.

Despite severe persecutions, Muhammad laid the foundation of a great new civilization—the Islamic civilization. During Muhammad's lifetime, the relationship between Islam, the religion founded by Muhammad, and Christianity was very good. Muhammad protected the

Christians, their churches, their priests, bishops and monks. When Imam 'Ali attempted to assert his position as Muhammad's verbally designated successor `Umar said "the Book of God is sufficient unto us". Because of this statement there was no written testament which led immediately to division, tribal jealousies, and personal ambitions arising. This short statement has echoed through the centuries. 'Abdu'l-Bahá, describes its woeful consequences, saying that

> "this statement caused the foundation of the religion of God in the Islamic Dispensation to be shattered and the ignoble worshippers of self and passion to rule over the righteous souls. It became a deadly weapon by which the Imam 'Ali himself was martyred, which caused great divisions within the nation of Islam and which changed the loving spirit of that nation to one of armed warriors. In His Tablet 'Abdu'l-Bahá explains that as a result of this statement Imam Husayn, the most illustrious of the Imams, was decapitated on the plain of Karbila, the other holy Imams were inflicted with great suffering, imprisonment and death, and the blood of countless innocent souls was shed for almost twelve hundred years."

— Adib Taherzadeh: The Child of the Covenant, p. 40

Islam was divided. The killing of Ali, Muhammad's cousin and son in law, in 661 A.D. opened the door for the powerful Umayyad tribe to rule Islam as an Arab empire, with little regard for religion or the teachings of Muhammad. The Umayyad tribe further destroyed the spirit of Islam. Instead of fostering brotherhood with the Christians they created hatred between the Christian civilization in the West and the new Islamic civilization in the East. Every history book will tell you how Christians and Muslims fought for hundreds of years resulting in the killing of millions of people during religious wars, called the 'crusades'. History records that the Christian church promised the people a direct entrance into Heaven if they killed Muslims during the crusades.[2] Those battles prevented the establishment of the unity in brotherhood that was the desire of both Jesus and Muhammad.

Islam – and the Book of Revelation

The dramatic story of the birth of Islam, the rise of Muhammad and the spiritual death of Islam is foretold in the Book of Revelation. The coming of Muhammad and Islam is described in highly symbolic language in chapters 11, 12 and 13 as:

"a great wonder in heaven, a woman clothed with the sun, and the moon under her feet, and upon her head a crown of twelve stars."

— Revelation 12:1

In many Biblical texts, a woman, often a bride, represents the Law of God. The sun and the moon are symbols for Persia and Turkey, the two countries that were under the shadow of that law. The crown of twelve stars upon her head are the twelve Imams who were the teachers of the Law of Muhammad.

"And she being with child, cried."

— Revelation 12:2

This shows us that the Law of Muhammad fell into the greatest difficulties and endured great trouble until the perfect child was born. Who caused the problems? It was the Umayyad tribe represented by the beast. John tells us this in symbolic language:

"... the dragon stood before the woman which was ready to be delivered, for to devour her child as soon as it was born."

— Revelation 12:4

Suddenly, the author of the Book of Revelation, John jumped further in time when he foretold events that would occur exactly 1,260 years later in another country:

"... that they should feed her there a thousand two hundred and threescore days."

— Revelation 12:6

One day in biblical terms represents one year: One score is 20 days. *"I have appointed thee each day for a year."* (Ezekiel, 4:6) and *"each day for a year"*. (Numbers, 14:34) This means that 1,260 years after Muhammad, the perfect child would be born. The year 1260 after Muhammad is the year 1844 of the Christian calendar. The Bahá'í era begins on this date. Therefore the perfect child is the coming of the Bahá'í Faith, announced by the Báb.

"Therefore rejoice ye heavens and ye that dwell in them."

— Revelation, 12:12

John asks us to rejoice in the coming of the new era, the new heaven, the beginning of the Bahá'í era.

John repeats in Chapter 12, the same vision of the woman with child; the child is now nourished for:

"... a time, and times, and half a time ..."

— Revelation, 12:14

This is three times and half a time, or three years and half a year, or 42 months, or (when one day equals one year) 1,260 years (42 × 30 = 1,260). This brings us again to the year 1260 after Muhammad, the beginning of the Bahá'í era! That the same term "a time, times, and half a time" was also used in Daniel 12:7, and this, together with the number 1,260, convinced most Bible scholars that their method of calculation was correct.

Consider how the prophecies correspond exactly with each other. The complete agreement between the prophecies of Daniel as referred to by Jesus and now again in the Book of Revelation is not a coincidence. This is very exciting, as the coming of Bahá'u'lláh fulfils the prophecies of the Jews, the Christians and the Muslims. These are three different religions, whose followers often opposed each other. The Bahá'í writings tell us:

> *"There are no clearer proofs than this in the Holy Books for any Manifestation."*
>
> — 'Abdu'l-Bahá: *Some Answered Questions*, p. 71

Biblical importance of the year 1844

In Chapter Eleven of the Book of Revelation there are additional references to the year 1260 A.H. of the Islamic calendar, which is the year 1844 in the Christian calendar:

> *"and the holy city shall they [the Gentiles] tread under foot forty and two months."*
>
> — Revelation, 11:2

As we discussed earlier, 42 months is 42 times 30 days, 1,260 days or 1,260 years:

> *"my two witnesses, and they shall prophesy a thousand two hundred and threescore days, clothed in sackcloth."*
>
> — *Revelation, 11:3*

> *"... the beast ... shall overcome them, and kill them. ... nations shall see their dead bodies three days and a half, and shall not suffer their dead bodies to be put in graves."*
>
> — Revelation 11:7 and 9

The beast is again the Umayyad tribe that will destroy the spirit of the teachings of Muhammad. The dead bodies that could not be buried means that the religion of God would be dead. The spirit of the religion, the fundamental principles that teach its morals, rules of conduct and the knowledge of God, were lost. Only the outer appearance and laws, such as prayer and fasting, would remain. This condition would last for 1,260 years or until the year 1844.

Again we find a reference to the three days and a half, bringing us to 1844:

"... after three days and a half the Spirit of life from God entered in them [the dead bodies] ..."

— Revelation, 11:11

The year 1844 marks the beginning of the Bahá'í Faith.[3]

"For him who is just, the agreement of the times indicated by the tongues of the Great Ones is the most conclusive proof. There is no other explanation of these prophecies."

— 'Abdu'l-Bahá: Some Answered Questions, p. 71

Conclusion

John not only foretold events occurring within Christianity, but also the coming of other new Messengers of God and the opposition to the plan of God. The power struggle of the leaders of religion against the new Messenger of God is symbolized by dragons, devils and beasts.

Let us now consider the glorious events that are occurring today. John mentions them over and over again using different expressions and symbols, because they are really important.

Clear indications for 1844 as the beginning of a new era, the Bahá'í Era, are found in the Book of Revelation more than six times. The coming of Bahá'u'lláh is the fulfilment of the Kingdom of God on earth. St. John describes this joyful event as follows:

"... great voices in Heaven, saying,

'The kingdoms of this world are become the kingdoms of our Lord, and of his Christ; and he shall reign for ever and ever.'"

— Revelation 11.15

The appearance of the Báb and Bahá'u'lláh, is described again and again by John in the most glorious terms, with the most beautiful symbols:

- The birth of a child
- The coming of a new heaven on earth
- The coming of the Glory of God, (Bahá'u'lláh)
- The cleansing of the temple
- The return of life into the dead body of religion
- The descent of the new Jerusalem as a bride
- The opening of the heavens
- Voices from heaven announcing the coming of the Kingdom of God on earth;

"Then at last the call of the Kingdom was raised, the spiritual virtues and perfections were revealed, the Sun of Reality dawned, and the teachings of the Most Great Peace, of the oneness of the world of humanity and the universality of men, were promoted."

— Selections of the Writings of 'Abdu'l-Bahá, p. 285

6

Difference between a true or false Prophet

"But do not trust any and every spirit, my friends. Test the spirits, to see whether they are from God, for among those who have gone out into the world, there are many prophets falsely inspired."

— 1 John 4:1

There are many statements in the Bible warning people to be aware of false prophets. However this does not mean that we should not investigate the truth of their claims. The Bible teaches us to *"test the spirits, to see whether they are of God"*[4]

Jews believed that Jesus was a false prophet

Jesus was considered to be a false prophet by the religious leaders of His time. The majority of the people blindly followed the priests who rejected Jesus.

"And there was much muttering among the people about Him; While some said, 'He is a good man'; others said: 'No, he is leading the people astray.'"

— John 7:12

Only a few Jews had "opened their spiritual eyes" and believed in Jesus. Most Jews did not believe in Jesus of Nazareth because He did not fulfil their understanding of the prophecies concerning the Advent of the Messiah. They believed:

- The Messiah will sit upon the throne of David but where is the throne of the Nazarene? *"He will re-establish King David's throne"* (Isaiah 9:6)

- The Messiah will rule with a sword. Jesus did not even have a staff, let alone a sword. *"He will carry a sword and defeat the enemies"* (Isaiah 66:16)

- Daniel has promised that He will rule Israel, but Jesus is a carpenter and not of princely birth. *"He will rule over Israel"* (Micah 5:2)

Most Jews believed in a literal fulfilment of the prophecies. Therefore, they did not accept Jesus as the Messiah.

Why was Jesus crucified?

The Jews had been waiting for thousands of years for the Messiah to appear. When Jesus came and proclaimed that He was the Messiah or the Christ, the Jews were very angry with Him and called Him a false prophet. Why, because they expected the Messiah (which means the Christ) to come as a strong and glorious earthly king, who would deliver them from oppressors and again form a great independent kingdom of the Jews. He would be a descendent of David and bring the whole world under His rule. The Jews were looking for such a Saviour or Deliverer, particularly around the time of the Advent of Jesus.

When Jesus said, He was the Christ or the Messiah, the rulers among the Jews refused to accept him largely because He and the way of His coming were so completely different from what they expected. Therefore, they rejected Jesus as the awaited King and crucified Him. To mock Him, the following writing was placed on the cross. *"Jesus of Nazareth, the King of the Jews"*. (John 19:19)

Were there false prophets after Jesus?

Many false prophets claiming to be Messiah or the Christ arose after Jesus. Bar-Jesus is mentioned in the Book of Acts 13:6: *"they found a ... false prophet, a Jew, whose name was Barjesus"*. Another false prophet by the name of Bar-Kochba arose about one hundred years after the death of Jesus. While Jesus had very few followers during His life, this false prophet was hailed by all the Jews as a savoir. Bar-Kochba promised to destroy the Roman army and make Palestine (consisting of Judea and Israel) a free land again.

Although Jesus warned us not to follow false prophets, many Jews accepted Bar-Kochba blindly because he promised them what they wanted. As a result, the Romans destroyed Israel. More than half a million people were killed, thousands of villages wiped out and entire cities burned! All the Jews were obliged to leave Palestine, and from that time until 1844, Jews only lived outside of Palestine.

The Jews blindly followed a false prophet with their spiritual eyes closed, firmly believing in all his promises. The result was physical and spiritual catastrophe.

How can we recognize a false prophet?

Many people go to church and hear many promises. They are promised that if they follow the teachings of that particular denomination they will be saved.

Sometimes the term "false prophets" is misused. It is often claimed that other churches are falsely leading the people. Unfortunately, this divides the people and prevents them from looking independently for the truth.

If we want to investigate what is true or false we must investigate ourselves. As the Apostle Paul advises us in 1 Thessalonians 5:19–21: *"Quench not the Spirit. Despise not prophesying. Prove all things; hold fast that which is good."*

Jesus' standard of judging prophets

Jesus gave us a standard by which we can judge what is true or false without having to rely on the opinions of others.

Jesus said:

> *"Beware of false prophets. Ye shall know them by their fruits. Do men gather grapes of thorns or figs of thistles? Even so every good tree brings forth good fruit but a corrupt tree brings forth evil fruit. A good tree cannot bring forth evil fruit neither can a corrupt tree bring forth good fruits. Wherefore by the fruits ye shall know them."*

— Matt 7:15–20

Three times Jesus repeats the phrase "**the fruit is important**".

What does Jesus mean by fruits?

A tree is often used as a symbol for the Prophet or the Messenger of God. The fruits produced by a tree symbolize the teachings of the Messenger of God. If you study the teachings of Jesus, you will see that they are very good teachings or good fruit.

Similarly, when you study the teachings of Bahá'u'lláh, specially revealed for this time, you will conclude that His teachings will help you to develop spiritually. These teachings will also help to unite people from all denominations, religions, races, nations and cultures to create a better world therefore they are also good fruits. If the fruit is good, then the tree is good; if the teachings are good, the Prophet is true. That is the test. This was the case in the time of Jesus, and it is also the case now with the coming of Bahá'u'lláh. Using this test, judge for yourself whether Bahá'u'lláh brings good fruits or not.

Some teachings or fruits of Bahá'u'lláh

1. **God is One**, the **foundation of all Religions is one** and **Mankind is one**. This means that people of all races in reality belong to one human family and are equal in the sight of one God.

2. **Man must investigate truth for himself** and not blindly follow the customs, traditions and religions that vary from one country to another.

3. There is no inequality based on gender. **Men and women must have equal opportunities, rights and privileges**.

4. **An international language** should be taught in schools for everyone to learn along with the mother tongue. World communications will be facilitated when everyone knows this international language.

5. **All people** must receive a basic **education.**

6. **Everyone must** try very hard to **remove all the prejudices** that divide races, religions and cultures, and promote the unity of its people.

7. **Religion and science must agree** and complement each other: religion deals with our spiritual life and science deals with our material life.

8. Everyone must work to **end the extremes of wealth and poverty.** All people must have equal educational and economic opportunities, and equal access to decent living conditions. There is a spiritual solution to economic problems.

9. In the future there will be **World Peace.**

These teachings are but a few of the fruits of Bahá'u'lláh's writings. These **fruits are good fruits**, which help humankind. Already they have united millions of people worldwide who are from diverse races and different religious backgrounds.

When you study the life of Bahá'u'lláh, you will find many proofs of His Divine authority: His compassion for poor people, His innate wisdom and knowledge from the time He was a child, His accurate predictions, His perfect character manifested in a life of suffering, and His great contributions for moral education and social reform.

The antichrist

No discussion of false prophets is complete without mentioning 'the antichrist'.

Some churches believe in the coming of a sinister individual known as the 'antichrist' who will mislead Christians. Jesus never mentioned this and it is not found in the Gospels. This idea was developed in the early church and is only mentioned in a letter of John written at the end of the first century.

One of the greatest problems for the early church was the appearance of false teachers who denied the human and spiritual nature of Jesus Christ, and created new sects.

John exposed these false teachers and called them antichrists. The word 'antichrist' is only mentioned in three passages in the Bible.

In I John 2:18, John tells us that there is not one, but many antichrists: *"Little children ... there are many antichrists"*.

In I John 4:1–3, John explains the meaning of antichrist and tells us that the antichrist was already in the world soon after the death of Jesus.

"Every spirit that confesseth that Jesus Christ is come in

the flesh is of God: And every spirit that confesseth not that Jesus Christ is come in the flesh is not of God: and this is that spirit of antichrist, whereof ye have heard that it should come; and even now already is it in the world".

In II John 1:7, John confirms again how to recognize the antichrist. He tells us that the antichrist is *"Every spirit that confesseth not that Jesus Christ is come in the flesh. This is a deceiver and an antichrist."*

Churches have often used fear of the antichrist to turn people away from investigating truth. However, a minute of reflection will prove that Bahá'u'lláh glorifies Jesus, defends all of His claims and affirms the reality of Jesus' divine position as the 'Word made flesh'. Therefore, it is obvious that He cannot be the antichrist. His followers, called Bahá'ís, have a strong belief in Jesus the Christ, accept Jesus as the Son of God and testify to the truth of all that the Bible teaches about Jesus.

7

The new name

"Say, O followers of the Son [Jesus]! Have ye shut
out yourselves from Me by reason of My Name?"

— Tablets of Bahá'u'lláh, p. 9

Why a new name?

Initially we may find it strange that the new Manifestation of
God will have a new name. We are so used to the name of
Jesus Christ. However, in this day we should try not to be too
attached to His name. Jesus warned that false prophets would
come after Him using His name (Christ) to deceive people.

"For many shall come in my name saying, I am Christ
and shall deceive many."

— Mark 13:6, Matt. 24:5 and Luke 21:8

The Bible tells us that at His Return Christ will be called
by a new name. Many Christians will not like this idea.
However, we must be careful not to make the same mistake
as the Jews in Jesus' time who had never heard the name
Jesus. They only knew Moses. The name Jesus was not
mentioned in their Holy Writings.

"The Lord God ... shall call His servants by another
name."

— Isaiah 62:2

The Book of Revelation when referring to the Second
Coming of Christ promises that that He will have a new name.

"I will write upon him my new name"

— Revelation 3:12

"He who hath an ear, let him hear ... To him who overcometh will I give to eat of the hidden manna and will give him a white stone, and in the stone a new name written. He who hath an ear, let him hear..."

— Revelation 2:17

Both of these references are accompanied by the words: *"He who has an ear, let him hear"*. Both also emphasize that in order to recognize the new name one must struggle to overcome obstacles. An obstacle is the prejudice we typically feel towards any new and strange sounding name and a new identity.

The new identity

The Pharisees and the scribes especially pointed out to the people that the name Jesus did not appear in the Books of Moses or in any of the Jewish writings. The new name was also accompanied by a new identity. *"Is this not a carpenter's son?"* (Matt. 13:55)

He was coming from a place which had much less prestige. "Can anything good come out of Nazareth?"

— John 1:46

"Is the Christ to come from Galilee?"

— John 7:41

The Jews became angry when Jesus said he came from heaven and they muttered:

"Who is that man Jesus, we know his father?"

— John 6:42

"Is not his mother called Mary? And are not his brothers James and Joseph and Simon and Judas? And are not all his sisters with us? ... and they took offence at him"

— Matt. 13:55–57

The new name: Bahá'u'lláh, the Glory of God

When you heard for the first time the name Bahá'u'lláh did you think what a strange name? The name is Oriental, from the East. It is interesting to note that the name Bahá'u'lláh is clearly mentioned several times in both the Old and New Testaments, every time in connection with the Return of Christ and as a prophecy for important events that would occur during the life of Bahá'u'lláh. Bahá'u'lláh is an Arabic name that can be translated into English as the "Glory of God", "Glory of the Lord" or "Glory of the Father".

For those readers who are interested in Bible prophecies, we will list some of the quotations where the Glory of God is mentioned in the Bible together with significant events during the life of Bahá'u'lláh.

"For the Son of Man is to come with His angels in the Glory of His Father"

— Matt. 16:27

Several prophets in the Old Testament had visions about a Messenger of God coming from Persia and standing near a river, close to Baghdád. The name of this new Messenger is "The Glory of God". All those prophesies were fulfilled by Bahá'u'lláh, the Glory of God, in 1863 when He declared His Message to the world while in the vicinity of Baghdád, on an island in the midst of the river Tigris.

"And behold the Glory of the Lord stood there as the Glory which I saw by the river of Chebar and I fell on my face."

— Ezekiel 3:23

This quote from Ezekiel mentions not only the name of the new Messenger of God as the 'Glory of God', it also gives a place name: 'the river Chebar'. Where do we find this river? A detailed map of Iraq shows the river Chebar flows in the vicinity of Baghdád. In the time of Ezekiel (more than 2,500 years ago), modern Baghdád was not yet built. However, close to the present day Baghdád, we find the ruins of the ancient city of Babylon. Ezekiel tells us that he was in exile in Babylon (close to Baghdád) when he saw the appearance of God in a vision which he describes as the *"appearance of the likeness of the Glory of God."*

— Ezekiel 1:28

That Jesus and Bahá'u'lláh were different becomes clear from this vision of Stephen, the first Christian martyr. The first Christian martyr, Stephen, was accused by the religious authorities of blasphemy against Moses and God. In a moving speech, Stephen explained why he believed in Abraham, Moses and Jesus. This speech, recorded in the Bible, gives us an insight into the thinking of the first Jewish Christians before Christians of pagan background became the dominant voice heard in the Christian church. Before Stephen was stoned to death, he saw a vision in which Jesus and Bahá'u'lláh were standing at the right hand of God.

"But he, full of the Holy Spirit, gazed into heaven and saw the Glory of God and Jesus standing on the right hand of God" *(Acts 7:55)*

Also Isaiah spoke about the Glory of the Lord.

"And the Glory of the Lord shall be revealed"

— Isaiah 40:5

Bahá'u'lláh was exiled from Persia to Palestine (Israel). You will see on the map on page 72 that Iran is positioned east of Israel. Ezekiel recorded his vision of the last days saying:

"And behold, the Glory of the Lord of Israel came from the way of the East"

— Ezekiel 43:1

In another verse, Ezekiel says:

*"And behold, the Glory of the Lord came into the
house by way of the gate, whose prospect is towards
the East"*

— Ezekiel 43:4

The name Bahá'u'lláh (The Glory of God) is mentioned
several times in the Book of Revelation with reference to
the coming of the City of God, the New Jerusalem For
example:

*"And showed me the Holy city the new Jerusalem,
descending out of Heaven, having **the Glory of
God**: and her light was like unto a stone most
precious"*

· — Revelation 21:10-11

What is the meaning of Jerusalem coming down from
Heaven? The coming of the city of God, a new Jerusalem,
from heaven cannot be literally understood.

*"And I John saw the holy city, new Jerusalem coming
down from Heaven, prepared as a bride adorned for
her husband."*

— Revelation 21:2

It is very clear that cities do not fall out of Heaven. Cities
are built up from the ground with much effort. Therefore, a
literal interpretation makes no sense! How could a city be
adorned as a bride? Therefore, the "city of God" has a spiritual
meaning. The new Jerusalem is the "Word of God", the new
teachings brought by the "Return of Christ".

"Behold I make all things new"

— Revelation 21:5

Elsewhere in the New Testament the name Bahá'u'lláh
is also mentioned.

> *"And the city had no light of the sun, neither of the moon to shine in it: for **the Glory of God** did lighten it."*

— Revelation 21:23

The sun and the moon are the symbols for spiritual guidance. The spiritual guide (or light) for the New Jerusalem is "**the Glory of God**".

Some prophecies even mention Bahá'u'lláh, the Glory of God, when He was a prisoner in 'Akká, near the valley of Sharon and the mountain Carmel in the Holy Land.

> *"The excellence of Carmel and Sharon; they shall see the Glory of the Lord and the excellency of our God."*

— Isaiah 35:1

The place of His Coming

Many Bible scholars were surprised that so many of the prophecies that had not been fulfilled by the coming of Jesus, pointed to the Persian Empire as the place of His second Coming

Mr. H. Bonar, a Christian scholar writing on Biblical prophecy in the early part of the nineteenth century, accepted the prophecies about Assyria, Elam and Persia, but he confessed that he was unable to explain why these places should, "in the latter days" be so blessed. For example, in Jeremiah 49:38 we read that God promised: *"I will set my throne in Elam"*. Also Daniel 8:2 and Ezekiel 1:28 gives "the province of Elam" as the place of the vision for the time of the end. Daniel prophesied from Shushan,[5] the capital city of Elam (which is now called Iran) and mentions in Daniel 8:2 that *"Elam would be given as a place of vision in the latter days"*.

Both the Báb and Bahá'u'lláh fulfilled these prophesies as they were born in Iran, which was called Elam at the time when Daniel wrote the prophecy.

Other prophesies fulfilling events in the life of Bahá'u'lláh

Bahá'u'lláh fulfilled many other prophecies related to the Second Coming. To understand this we have to study the significant events in the life of Bahá'u'lláh.

In this introduction to the topic we will look at only one paragraph in one small book from the Bible called the book of Micah. In this book, we find many prophecies that present a picture where all the pieces fit together. Some are related to the life of Jesus[6], others to the life of Bahá'u'lláh.

"In that day also he shall come even to thee from Assyria, and from the fortified cities, and from the fortress even to the river, and from sea to sea, and from mountain to mountain. Notwithstanding the land will be desolate ... Feed thy people with thy rod ... in the midst of Carmel ... According to the days of thy coming out of the land of Egypt will I show unto him marvellous things. The nations shall see ... they shall lay their hand upon their mouth, their ears will be deaf."

— Micah 7:12–15

[1] *"He shall come from Assyria"*

Bahá'u'lláh was born in Tihrán, the capital city of Iran or Persia, which was located in the ancient Assyrian Empire.

[2] *"... from the fortified cities"*

Bahá'u'lláh was taken in chains from the fortified city of Constantinople to the fortress city of 'Akká. (see map on page 72). Bahá'u'lláh was imprisoned in the fortress city of

'Akká. This fortress was so well built that even the French emperor Napoleon Bonaparte was unable to capture it. He left cannonballs buried in the thick stone walls as a memory of his futile attempt.

[3] *"... from the fortress to the river"*

After being released from the fortress of 'Akká Bahá'u'lláh went to the small island (also named the Ridván Garden) in the Na'mayin River just to the south of 'Akká. There He spent many hours and welcomed those who sought His counsel.

[4] *"... from sea to sea"*

During His exile and banishment Bahá'u'lláh was sent from the Black Sea in Turkey to the Mediterranean Sea on whose shores the prison-fortress of 'Akká is located.

[5] *"... from mountain to mountain"*

Bahá'u'lláh withdrew for two years to the remote Mount Galú in Iraq. Later He was banished to 'Akká close to Mount Carmel, on whose slopes he spent His last years.

[6] *"... the land shall be desolate"*

When Bahá'u'lláh arrived in 'Akká after a miserable sea journey the entire population of the city was filled with hatred for Him since the religious leaders had lied to the people telling them that Bahá'u'lláh was a criminal and an enemy of Islam. Not only was the land spiritually desolate, but it also was filled with physical desolation, typhoid, malaria, diphtheria and dysentery. (Soon after the arrival of Bahá'u'lláh in 'Akká, the climate in 'Akká started to gradually improve. The winds changed direction. When a leader of 'Akká, who respected Bahá'u'lláh, asked Him what he could do for Him, Bahá'u'lláh asked him to restore an old aqueduct. The leader obeyed the prisoner and soon fresh water was once again available for the population. Today, 'Akká is a healthy place for people to live.)

[7] *"Feed thy people ... in the midst of Carmel"*

Bahá'u'lláh was imprisoned very close to Mount Carmel. During one of His visits after He was released He pitched His tent on the slopes of Mount Carmel. It was there that He revealed The Tablet of Carmel in which He spoke of the Glory of this Holy Spot. His words were like spiritual food to edify the souls of men.

[8] *"According to the days of thy coming out of Egypt will I show unto Him marvellous things."*

"The days of thy coming out of the land of Egypt" means the period the Jews were wandering through the desert under the guidance of Moses after leaving Palestine. The Bible tells us that after forty years the Jews finally reached the Holy land, Palestine.

Just like Moses, after Bahá'u'lláh was released from the prison in Tihrán He began a forty year period of exile and further imprisonments. His sufferings ended only with His Ascension in the Holy Land in 1892. Hence, from the beginning of His mission in 1852 until the last days of His life there passed forty years of suffering and revelation exactly "according the days of Moses coming out of the land of Egypt".

[9] *"The nations shall see ... they shall lay their hand upon their mouth, their ears will be deaf."*

Bahá'u'lláh wrote letters to all the great leaders of the nations of His time but received little response from most of them. As Micah prophesied, the great kings laid their hands upon their mouths and their ears were deaf.

Fulfilment of prophecies

The new name, the place and time of His coming have all been foretold in the Bible. Man's planning is futile when confronted with the plans of God.

The reason why the clergy and government officials banished Bahá'u'lláh to 'Akká was because they hoped that He would die quickly in that desolate prison and not be heard of again. As an exile and a prisoner Bahá'u'lláh fulfilled the prophecies of Isaiah, Ezekiel and Hosea, who had visions of "the Glory of God" appearing in Persia and coming to 'Akká in the Holy Land;

Indeed

> *"The promises of God, as recorded in the Holy Scriptures, have all been fulfilled."*

> — *Gleanings from the Writings of Bahá'u'lláh*, p. 13

8

How will we recognize
the Messenger of God?

"... whoso looketh for Christ in His physical body hath looked in vain, and will be shut away from Him as by a veil. ... In this new and wondrous day, it behoveth thee to seek after the spirit of Christ."

— *Selections from the Writings of 'Abdu'l-Bahá*, p. 167

Some people think that when the Christ returns they will be able to recognize Him physically. They expect to see the same bodily form of Jesus who walked the streets of Jerusalem two thousand years ago.

The Bible does not give us any physical details of Jesus' appearance. The existing paintings of Jesus are according to the imagination of the artists[7]

Jesus Himself gave some signs that would enable us to recognize Him at the time of His return which can be summarized as follows:

• The promised One will speak with the same voice as Jesus.

• He shall glorify and bear witness of Jesus.

• He will explain Jesus' words.

He will speak with the same voice

Jesus gave the following sign to His disciples when they asked Him how they would recognize the Promised One. Using a symbolic language Jesus compared His followers with sheep. He said:

"My sheep hear my voice and I know them and they follow Me."

— John 10:27

Would you recognize the voice of Jesus when He returns? No one alive today knows His voice. Therefore, it is clear that we are not thinking of the voice itself but rather what He has to say i.e. His teachings. Bahá'u'lláh revealed more than one hundred books. Anybody who studies these books will conclude that there is no contradiction between the 'voice' or teachings of Bahá'u'lláh and the 'voice' or teachings of Jesus both of which are the Word of God. Bahá'u'lláh speaks with the same voice as Jesus but has addressed the issues of the people in our time. Jesus was a good teacher and addressed the needs and level of the people of His time. Bahá'u'lláh speaks about the problems of the whole world as we now know it.

There is no conflict between the words of Jesus and the words of Bahá'u'lláh. Both complement each other. For example, Jesus said to love your neighbour and now Bahá'u'lláh says to love mankind.

He shall glorify and bear witness of Jesus

Jesus Himself promised that the Promised One would glorify Christ. In John 16:14, Jesus said: "He will glorify Me ..." and in John 15:26: "He will bear witness to Me".

Bahá'u'lláh glorified Jesus in His Writings. For example, Bahá'u'lláh proclaimed:

"This is that which the Son [Jesus] hath decreed" And whatsoever hath proceedeth out of His blameless, His truth-speaking, trustworthy mouth, can never be altered."

— *Tablets of Bahá'u'lláh*, p. 14

Bahá'u'lláh glorified Christ:

"He [Christ] it is Who purified the world. Blessed is the man who, with a face beaming with light, hath turned towards Him."

— *Gleanings from the Writings of Bahá'u'lláh*, p. 86

Bahá'u'lláh wrote about the crucifixion of Jesus:

"Know thou that when the Son of Man yielded up His breath to God, the whole creation wept with a great weeping. By sacrificing Himself, however, a fresh capacity was infused into all created things. Its evidences, as witnessed in all the peoples of the earth, are now manifest before thee."

— *Gleanings from the Writings of Bahá'u'lláh*, p. 85

Bahá'u'lláh linked His own life with that of Jesus Christ throughout His mission. After having suffered stoning, poisoning, torture and imprisonment, Bahá'u'lláh lifted up His voice to cry out:

"O Jews! If ye be intent on crucifying once again Jesus, the Spirit of God, put Me to death, for He hath once more, in My person, been made manifest unto you. Deal with Me as ye wish, for I have vowed to lay down My life in the path of God."

— *Gleanings from the Writings of Bahá'u'lláh*, p. 101

He will explain the words of Jesus

Jesus said: *"He will take of mine and show it unto you"* (John 16:15)

Bahá'u'lláh explained many verses of the Bible that for centuries had confused and divided Christianity. He confirms that Jesus is the Son of God, explains the mystery of the Trinity, the meaning of resurrection, the day of judgement and many other statements.

Bahá'u'lláh, the new Manifestation of God

A new Messenger of God has appeared who fulfils all the conditions given by Jesus for His Return. His name is Bahá'u'lláh, which means the Glory of God! His words bring the same wisdom as the words of Jesus, as they both spoke with the same divine inspiration and both had the same heavenly power. Both suffered greatly from persecution. Large numbers of their first followers were mocked, imprisoned, tortured and executed in public in the most horrible fashion. Just as the Christian martyrs had the choice of denying Jesus and thereby saving their lives; so too the Bahá'í martyrs had the choice of renouncing Bahá'u'lláh or to die for their love of Him.

Bahá'u'lláh lived a life of sacrificial devotion to God, upholding the Teachings of Jesus Christ and the Bible.

Bahá'u'lláh wrote:

"... Jesus, the Spirit of God ... hath once more, in My person, been made manifest unto you."

— *Gleanings from the Writings of Bahá'u'lláh*, p. 101

"He who is the Lord of Lords is come overshadowed with clouds. ... He, verily, hath again come down from Heaven even as He came down from it the first time."

— *The Summons of the Lord of Hosts*, p. 54–5

"Beware lest ye dispute that which He proclaimeth, even as the people before you disputed His utterances."

— *Tablets of Bahá'u'lláh*, p. 11

"The time foreordained unto the peoples and kindreds of the earth," affirms Bahá'u'lláh, *"is now come. The promises of God, as recorded in the Holy Scriptures, have all been*

fulfilled.... This is the Day which the Pen of the Most High hath glorified in all the Holy Scriptures. There is no verse in them that doth not declare the glory of His holy Name, and no Book that doth not testify unto the loftiness of this most exalted theme"

— Shoghi Effendi: *The Promised Day is Come*, p. 76

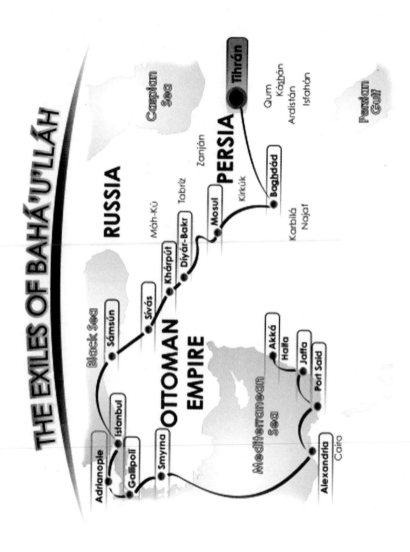

The exiles of Baha'u'llah

9

Life and sufferings of Bahá'u'lláh

"Whoso will reflect upon the tribulations We have suffered, his soul will assuredly melt away in sorrow. ... We have sustained the weight of all calamities to sanctify you from all earthly corruption, and ye are yet indifferent."

— Gleanings from the Writings of Bahá'u'lláh, p. 307

Youth of Bahá'u'lláh

Bahá'u'lláh was born on 12 November 1817 in Tihrán, Persia, now called Iran. His family had wealth and social position. Bahá'u'lláh's father was an important minister in the court of the Shah of Iran.

Bahá'u'lláh was different from other children. Despite the fact that he did not attend school he had an unusual knowledge and deep spiritual perception. From earliest childhood, He had an extraordinary power of attracting people to Him. By the time He was thirteen he was well known for His learning and people came to Him to solve their problems. Like Jesus He could talk on any subject, and explain difficult religious questions and the leading priests would listen with great interest. — Luke 2:46)

When Bahá'u'lláh was twenty-two his father died. He was offered His father's position as a minister in the government. To the astonishment of those in the court of the

Shah Bahá'u'lláh refused this influential post. Many people, rich and poor, educated and illiterate, knew of Bahá'u'lláh and they loved, respected and wondered about Him. He was known as the 'father of the poor' and his wife Ásíyih Khánum as `the mother of consolation'. They both spent their time helping the oppressed, the sick and the poor and championing the cause of justice. 'Abdu'l-Bahá, His eldest son was born on 23rd May 1844, the same moment that the Báb declared His mission to Mullá Husayn.

Bahá'u'lláh in prison

The respect that was shown to Bahá'u'lláh turned into anger and hate when at the age of twenty–seven He became a follower of the Báb. The believers in the Báb were called Bábís. Thousands of Bábís were tortured and killed under terrible circumstances. Bahá'u'lláh's high social standing did not prevent Him from being persecuted along with the other Bábís. His first imprisonment was when He was helping Táhirih's companions. The second time was when He was on His way to join those who were defending themselves at Fort of Shaykh-Tabarsi. This time He was put in prison, no doubt, by the Will of God, to protect Him from being killed when all the rest of those heroes were killed in the cruel slaughter. On this occasion, Bahá'u'lláh was pelted with stones by a mob, insulted, and He suffered the bastinado (being beaten on the soles of the feet until they bled severely).

After the martyrdom of the Báb, Bahá'u'lláh was taken prisoner for the third time. He was force-marched, barefoot and bareheaded in the fierce summer sun, from Shimírán to the dungeon in Tihrán, a distance of approximately fifteen kilometres. Along the road a big crowd had gathered to jeer and heap insults on Him. An old woman was seen to emerge from the midst of the crowd with a stone in her hand, eager to cast it in the face of Bahá'u'lláh, but was having trouble catching up the party. Bahá'u'lláh stopped His escorts saying, *"Suffer not this woman to be disappointed. Deny her not what she regards as a meritorious act in the sight of God."*[8] Such was His compassion and understanding.

People had done the same to Jesus. On a day that is now commemorated by Christians as Palm Sunday, the people of Jerusalem had gone out to greet Him and had said *"Hosanna to the Son of David; Blessed is He"* (Matt. 21:9). Yet few days later they jeered and reviled Him and yelled out *"Crucify Him"*.

Bahá'u'lláh was imprisoned in an underground dungeon called the "Black Pit" in Teheran together with other Bábí's. A chain weighing over fifty kilograms was placed around His neck, the scars of which were with Him to the end of His life. The prison was dark and icy-cold, dirty and filthy and crawling with insects. The smell was foul beyond belief. The Shah's mother arranged for some of Bahá'u'lláh's food to be poisoned, so strong was her hatred towards Him. Although the poison did not kill Bahá'u'lláh it left Him with poor health for many years of His life.

Bahá'u'lláh had been hurled into that black hole and was chained day and night to the other Bábís. Imagine the horror of these conditions. Any movement caused the chain to cut deeper and deeper into the flesh of all those who were chained together. Sleep or rest was not possible. Every day the executioners would come to the dungeon and call out the names of those who would be tortured to death. They would be given to different classes of people in the city. The butchers would use their knives on them, the bakers would put their feet or their heads into their ovens, the shoemakers and the blacksmiths would make them suffer with their tools of the trade.

Revelation from God

Each of the Divine Messengers received the Announcement of His Prophetic Mission in a special way. Just as the dove had descended upon Jesus in the river Jordan, and the Burning Bush had appeared to Moses, so did the Most Great Spirit appear to Bahá'u'lláh. He wrote of that experience, saying:

"By my life! Not of Mine own volition have I revealed Myself, but God, of His own choosing, hath manifested Me...Whenever I chose to hold My peace and be still, lo, the Voice of the Holy Spirit, standing on My right hand, aroused Me...and the Spirit of Glory stirred within My bosom, bidding Me arise and break My silence."

— Shoghi Effendi, *God Passes By*, p. 102

Bahá'u'lláh wrote an account of those hours when He became conscious of His Divine Mission:

"During the days I lay in the prison of Tihrán, though the galling weight of the chain and the stench-filled air allowed Me but little sleep, still in those infrequent moments of slumber I felt as if something flowed from the crown of My head over My breast, even as a mighty torrent that precipitateth itself upon the earth from the summit of a lofty mountain. Every limb of My body would, as a result, be set afire. At such moments My tongue recited what no man could bear to hear."

— Bahá'u'lláh: *Epistle to the Son of the Wolf*, p. 22

"One night in a dream, these exalted words were heard on every side: 'Verily, We shall render Thee victorious by Thyself and by Thy pen. Grieve Thou not for that which hath befallen Thee, neither be Thou afraid, for Thou art in safety."

— Bahá'u'lláh: *Epistle to the Son of the Wolf*, p. 21

"While engulfed in tribulations I heard a most wondrous, a most sweet voice, calling above My head. Turning My face, I beheld a Maiden. Pointing with her finger unto My head, she addressed all who are in heaven and all who are on earth, saying: By God! This is the Best-Beloved of the worlds, and yet ye comprehend not. This is the Beauty of God amongst you, and the power of His sovereignty within you, could ye but understand. This is the Mystery of God and His Treasure, the Cause of God and His glory unto all who are in the kingdoms of Revelation and of creation, if ye be of them that perceive."

— Bahá'u'lláh: *The Summons of the Lord of Hosts*, pp. 5–6

Bahá'u'lláh banished from Iran

The Russian Counsel rose up in the Court of the Shah and said; "Beware! If one hair of his head is hurt from this moment on, rivers of blood shall flow in your town as a punishment. You will do well to listen to my warning, my country is behind me in this matter." On His release, the Shah ordered Bahá'u'lláh and His family to immediately leave Iran. In the bitter cold of winter, with no proper clothes or supplies, they were sent as exiles to the city of Baghdád, in Iraq. They all suffered terribly. Their route crossed mountainous parts of Iran where thick ice and snow covered the ground. They travelled for three months in the heart of winter from

12 January 1853 to 8 April the same year. A guard and a Russian official accompanied them. When one thinks about the way in which Bahá'u'lláh was forced to leave His native land, one is reminded of what happened to other Messengers of God – how Muhammad was forced to leave Mecca and move to Medina, how Mary and Joseph had to flee from Bethlehem into Egypt with Jesus, how Moses led His brother and His followers out of the land of Egypt and how Abraham was forced out of Ur to the Promised Land.

First stop: Baghdád

Baghdád, the capital of Iraq which is situated on the banks of the Tigris River was the first stage of Bahá'u'lláh's forty years of forced exile. Under the gentle guiding influence of Bahá'u'lláh the Bábí community in Baghdad began once again to blossom. But like Judas Iscariot who was consumed by jealousy for the rising spiritual influence of Christ, Mírzá Yahyá the half-brother of Bahá'u'lláh began to sow fear and suspicion in the pure soil of those believers' hearts. Soon arguments arose amongst the community members in the same way that arguments had arisen amongst the disciples of Jesus and the descendants of Muhammad. These differences of opinion were very painful to Bahá'u'lláh whose purpose was to bring unity to the people of the world, so to avoid disunity on 10 April 1854 He removed Himself by suddenly leaving Baghdád with no intention of returning. He left expecting

"no return and no reunion" "The one object of Our retirement was to avoid becoming a subject of discord among the faithful, a source of disturbance unto Our companions, the means of injury to any soul, or the cause of sorrow to any heart"

— Bahá'u'lláh, *Kitáb-i-Íqán*, p. 251

Bahá'u'lláh in the wilderness

The Bible tells us about the forty days that Jesus Christ spent in prayer and fasting, alone in the desert before He was ready to preach the Gospel. For Bahá'u'lláh the two years in the mountainous regions of Sulaymáníyyih were his last days of peace and His preparation for forty years of Revelation.

In the wilderness He lived alone as a hermit in a cave and spent all His time in prayer and meditation. Nobody knew His identity or His origin. However, just as the sun and its radiance cannot be hidden from the sight of men, so also the greatness and glory of Bahá'u'lláh could not be hidden from the eyes of those who met Him. Two years later news reached Baghdád that a Holy Person was living in Sulaymáníyyih and His family knew that this must be Bahá'u'lláh. They sent a messenger to beg Him to return, which He did on the 19 March 1856.

Under the wise leadership of Bahá'u'lláh the Bábí community once again started to thrive and grow. As the popularity of Bahá'u'lláh and the number of believers increased, so did the jealousy of the Mullahs. Every day He lived with the uncertainty of whether He would be allowed to live any longer. The Islamic clergy and learned people were always questioning Him about His beliefs. Plots were made against Him, for example, a cold blooded murderer, Ridá Turk, was hired to kill Bahá'u'lláh. Ridá Turk twice attempted to kill Bahá'u'lláh, but twice he was overcome with such fear, awe and remorse, that his hands trembled and his gun fell to the ground.

A royal prince visited Bahá'u'lláh and said "I know not how explain it. Were all the sorrows of the world to be crowded into my heart, they would, I feel, all vanish when in the presence of Bahá'u'lláh. It is as if I had entered Paradise itself."

Declaration in the garden of Paradise

The religious leaders were very worried about the influence Bahá'u'lláh had on the people, and they made false accusations about Him to the Shah in Persia. Finally Bahá'u'lláh was forced to leave Baghdád. As soon as the news spread that Bahá'u'lláh was leaving large groups of people came to bid their last farewell in a garden, which is now called the garden of Ridván. It is in this garden that Bahá'u'lláh openly declared that He was the Promised One of All Ages—He was that Great Teacher promised in all the Holy Books of the world. For twelve days, from 21st April to 2nd May 1863 Bahá'u'lláh received people into His presence. Of that time He said:

"all created things were immersed in the sea of Purification"

— Bahá'u'lláh, *Kitáb-i-Aqdas*, p. 48

As in the time of Jesus with people spreading palm branches to welcome Jesus, the believers piled roses in the centre of the floor of His blessed tent. As Bahá'u'lláh rode away thousands of people watched Him go. People bowed to the dust at the feet of His horse and kissed its hooves. Some even threw themselves in front of the horse wishing to be killed rather than be parted from their Beloved.

Again Bahá'u'lláh was banished by the plotting of His enemies and started the long journey to Constantinople, which was the capital of the Ottoman Empire, now called Turkey. He stayed in Constantinople only four months. Here He began to announce His Mission to the rest of the world starting with the Sultan of Turkey. The Persian Government continued its persecution from Iran and this resulted in His third exile, this time to Adrianople, under escort and with no time to prepare for the bitter cold of the hazardous winter journey which was the most terrible they had experienced.

Proclamation to the kings and rulers of the world

This proclamation to the kings and rulers marked the third stage of the unfoldment of His Mission. The first stage was in the "Black Pit" when the Divine Spirit announced to Him that He was the bearer of God's Message for this day. The second stage was His public proclamation to His believers in the Garden of Ridván in Baghdad. And the third stage was the universal proclamation to the kings, world and religious leaders – openly proclaiming His Mission to mankind.

In those letters Bahá'u'lláh proclaimed in clear and unmistakable language that the long-awaited age of world peace and brotherhood had as last dawned. He also gave warnings of the consequences if mankind turns away from this path of peace. For example, Bahá'u'lláh prophesied in a letter to Kaiser Wilhelm I that if Germany did not stop accumulating arms, then the banks of the Rhine would run with blood, not once but twice. This prophecy was fulfilled when Germany was defeated during the two world wars.

Bahá'u'lláh prophesied that Napoleon III, who at that time was the most powerful monarch in Europe, would be humbled.

"For what thou hast done, thy kingdom shall be thrown into confusion, and thine empire shall pass from thine hands, as a punishment for that which thou hast wrought."

— Bahá'u'lláh: *The Summons of the Lord of Hosts*, p. 72

And it happened exactly as Bahá'u'lláh had foretold.

As another example, let us take Bahá'u'lláh's letter to Pope Pius IX, asking him not to make the same mistake that the Jews had made in the days of Jesus Christ and turn away from His

Message. He asked the Pope to abandon his palaces and sell his treasures to help the poor people. The Pope paid no attention to this letter. Later he was forced to surrender to the Italian army that occupied Rome in 1870. As a result, Pope Pius IX became a prisoner in the Vatican.[9] (It is noteworthy that 1870 was also the year in which the Pope first proclaimed the controversial new dogma of Papal Infallibility)

Most Christians know that Jesus prophesied the destruction of Jerusalem. In a similar way Bahá'u'lláh prophesied many of the events that would profoundly influence and shape world history.

It was in Constantinople that Mírzá Yahyá (named the antichrist of the Bahá'í Revelation by Shoghi Effendi) poisoned Bahá'u'lláh. He was so ill that the poison left Him with a shaking hand till the end of His life.

Finally the Shah of Iran and the Sultan of Turkey were instrumental again in banishing Bahá'u'lláh to a town in Palestine (Israel[10]) called 'Akká, a fortified city that was used as a prison at that time.

Bahá'u'lláh incarcerated in the fortress of 'Akká

On the last day of August 1868, after a long journey over land and sea, Bahá'u'lláh's family and some close companions were put ashore at the Sea Gate of 'Akká. This city had been chosen because the religious leaders believed that Bahá'u'lláh would soon die there. 'Akká at the time was full of filth and disease and it was a prison for the worst types of criminals. Prevailing winds and tides created a climate so unhealthy that a popular saying held: "that a bird which flew over 'Akká would fall dead".

This was also the city that Hosea called 'a door of hope' and of which Ezekiel had said,

*"Afterward he brought me to the gate, even the gate
that looketh toward the east: And, behold, the glory
of the God of Israel came from the way of the east..."*

— Ezekiel 43:1–2

Bahá'u'lláh and His followers were deprived of food and
drink on the first night of their arrival. They even begged for
water, but were refused. Due to hunger, thirst and filthy
conditions, several of His followers later died of various
diseases. Bahá'u'lláh gave the prison soldiers His own carpet
to sell and pay for the funeral expenses. However, the soldiers
took the carpet for themselves and threw the bodies into a
hole in the ground.

Many Bahá'ís came from Iran, walking for months,
hoping to meet their Beloved, but the guards refused to allow
them to enter the prison. The pilgrims would stand outside
the fortress for days hoping to catch a glimpse of the Blessed
Beauty from behind the iron bars of His prison cell. When
they saw Bahá'u'lláh waving a white handkerchief they would
return back home giving the glad tidings of Bahá'u'lláh's
safety and health to the anxious believers.

It was from this prison in 'Akká that Bahá'u'lláh's
Message would spread worldwide.

"For out of prison he cometh to reign"

— Ecclesiastes 4:14

Bahá'u'lláh, the King of Kings

The prison conditions in 'Akká were very bad and many
prisoners died. Bahá'u'lláh was held in a particularly rigorous
confinement. Although He was not allowed visitors this could
not thwart His purpose. In the same way that Jesus submitted
to the sacrifice of His life on the cross, so also was Bahá'u'lláh
content with the will of God and submitted to that Will,

offering Himself as a living sacrifice. A great tragedy occurred when His son Mírzá Mihdí, while pacing backwards and forwards on the prison roof, deeply immersed in prayer, fell through the skylight and was critically injured. The saintly youth begged that his death would be accepted as a sacrifice for the sake of those souls who were yearning to speak with Bahá'u'lláh. Spiritual forces were indeed set in motion which opened the doors for the conditions of the prisoners to improve and for Bahá'u'lláh to be allowed to receive His visitors.

The Bible tells us that the people who met Jesus were profoundly changed by the experience. Some people were irresistibly drawn to Jesus whilst others rejected Him. Nobody was unaffected. The same happened in Bahá'u'lláh's life. There are many reports from witnesses how complete strangers, unaware of His station, bowed before Him involuntarily; of high ranking officers becoming awestruck and speechless in His presence; and of jailers, who though instructed by their superiors to treat Him with contempt, became devoted admirers.

There are likewise many reports that speak of Bahá'u'lláh's awe-inspiring majesty and kingly dignity, of His piercing eyes that seemed to read ones very soul, and His melodious voice that carried divine authority.

Revelation of Bahá'u'lláh

Jesus Himself did not write down His teachings. His words come indirectly to us through the Gospels. Bahá'u'lláh, on the other hand, recorded a vast amount of His own teachings. Much of it He dictated to His secretaries. There are some original documents, written in His own hand, that are stored in the Bahá'í archives in Haifa. When the Revelation from God came to Him, the words just poured from His lips, and several secretaries worked day and night to record them. The speed of dictation was so fast that within two days Writings were revealed of more than two hundred and fifty pages! Bahá'u'lláh never made a mistake, never changed anything or repeated Himself. He would attach His seal to all transcripts after checking them. He used both Farsi, the language of Persia, and Arabic in such an eloquent style that many scholars wondered how a man who never attended school was able to achieve such a high standard of writing.[11]

Bahá'u'lláh remained in exile for forty years. During those years He revealed hundreds of passages. His divinely inspired Writings are God's greatest gift to humankind in this new age. The most important book, the Most Holy Book (The Kitáb-i-Aqdas) contains the laws of the Bahá'í Faith. He called for Houses of Justice to be established to guide the believers and maintain order and unity.

Bahá'u'lláh's Ascension

When Bahá'u'lláh was seventy five years old, He told the people that He wished "to depart from this world." He was being called to *"other dominions, whereon the eyes of the people of names have never fallen"*. (Shoghi Effendi: God Passes By, p. 221)

He passed away at dawn on 29 May 1892. For a week after His death, Bahá'ís, Muslims, Christians and Jews gathered around the burial place of Bahá'u'lláh to mourn the loss of a great Being.

The Covenant of Succession

In the past religions no clear guidance was given by the Messengers of God about whom the followers should turn to after Their death. This led to disagreements and the formation of sects and thus the religion became divided.

Bahá'u'lláh wrote in His Will and Testament that all Bahá'ís should turn to 'Abdu'l-Bahá after His passing, and to obey him and follow the example of his life. Only 'Abdu'l-Bahá was given the authority to interpret and explain the teachings of Bahá'u'lláh. Bahá'u'lláh designated 'Abdu'l-Bahá as the Centre of the Covenant of God.

In this way, there is no possibility for any Bahá'í to form a sect based on his own interpretation of the Bahá'í Writings. The Bahá'í Faith is now over one hundred and sixty years old and it remains undivided. This has never happened before in the history of mankind. The reason that the Bahá'í Faith remains as a single and undivided religion is the power of the Covenant. This firm and unshakeable Covenant of Succession demonstrates the greatness of the Bahá'í Revelation.

10

God's Great Covenant

*"But this shall be the covenant that I will make with
the house of Israel; After those days, saith the Lord, I
will put my law in their inward parts, and write it in
their hearts; and will be their God and they shall be
my people."*

— Jeremiah 31:33

A covenant is a contract between two sides, each of whom
has obligations to fulfil. God has made a Covenant with
man. The creation of man was achieved by love. God knew
his love for us therefore He created us. In the Hidden Words
Bahá'u'lláh says:

*"O son of Man! I loved thy creation, hence I created
thee. Wherefore, do thou love Me, that I may name
thy name and fill thy soul with the spirit of life."*

God tells us that He loves us and our part in the agreement is
to love Him otherwise His love cannot reach us and we will
be deprived of its benefits. This obligation of man to return
God's love is again reinforced in the following Hidden Word
when Bahá'u'lláh tells us:

*"O Son of Being! Love Me, that I may love thee. If
thou lovest Me not, my love can in no wise reach thee.
Know this, O servant."*

There is an old Christian picture showing Jesus knocking

on a door of someone's heart. This door has no handle to open it from the outside. It must be opened from the inside. This little illustration can be understood as the door being the entrance to our heart. God's love knocks on the outside wanting to come in, but we must open our heart from the inside. It takes our free will to do this. Once this first step is taken and we open our hearts to the influence of God's love, then the next step is to follow Him. This means we know God, love Him and follow His teachings, and this can only be done through knowledge of His Manifestations.

The Covenant is an agreement

The relationship of God with man in this Covenant is somewhat similar to the relationship between the principal of a school and the child. When a child goes to school for the first time he enters into a covenant or an agreement with the school principal. The motive of the principal is his love for the child and concern for his education. In this contract the principal promises to provide the means for the education of the child. He appoints teachers to teach, draws up an educational program and ensures for the child's well-being and development. The child's part in this covenant is to follow the instructions of the teacher and to learn every lesson that he is taught. It is through this process that the child acquires knowledge and develops his capacities and becomes endowed with intellectual and spiritual powers. As the child grows in learning and maturity the principal will appoint other teachers to contribute to his education. Man has to follow these teachings voluntarily and obey wholeheartedly in order to enable his soul to progress and attain spiritual qualities. As the body of man is bound by the laws of nature his soul is governed by the laws of the Covenant of God.[12]

First mention of the Covenant

In the book of Genesis, God addresses Noah in 6:18 *"With thee will I establish my Covenant and thou shalt come into the ark"*. It then states that Noah obeyed God according to all that God commanded him. Noah's obedience was rewarded with God's blessings and he was saved from the flood. The sign of this Covenant with God is symbolized by the rainbow:

"I have set my rainbow in the clouds, and it will be the sign of the covenant between me and the earth. Whenever I bring clouds over the earth and the rainbow appears in the clouds, I will remember my covenant between me and you and all living creatures of every kind."

— Genesis 9:13–15

The word Testament comes from a Latin word that means Covenant. Further mention of the Covenant was with Abraham.

Abraham was a descendant of one of the sons of Noah. Abraham is pictured in the Bible as the father of faith in God because of His faithful obedience to God's call. His greatest test came when He was called to sacrifice His son Isaac. God tested Abraham, Who demonstrated His willingness to obey, and thus received God's blessings:

"And I will establish my covenant between me and thee, and thy seed after thee in their generations, for an everlasting covenant, to be a God unto thee, and to thy seed after thee."

— Genesis 17:7

God made Abraham a promise that He would give Abraham's line many children and through Abraham's children, the world would be blessed. God made this promise nearly four thousand years ago.

The three wives of Abraham

On page 93 is a simplified lineage diagram.[23] The Bible tells us that Abraham had three wives: Sarah, Hagar and Katurah. (Gen. 12:29, 16:3 and 25:1) They gave Abraham a number of sons. Sarah is the mother of Isaac, Hagar gave birth to Ishmael and Katurah had six sons. These children of Abraham had their own children and so the lineage grew.

God kept his promise to Abraham. Moses, Jesus, Muhammad, the Báb and now Bahá'u'lláh are all descendants from the seed of Abraham. Bahá'u'lláh is, in the words of the Guardian:

"the Rod come forth out of the stem of Jesse" and the
"Branch grown out of His roots"

— Shoghi Effendi, *God Passes By*, p. 94

The simplified diagram mainly shows Bahá'u'lláh's lineage through Katurah. Bahá'u'lláh is also a descendant of Sarah via Jesse, the father of King David.

"Bahá'u'lláh is thus the descendant of Jesse, the father of David."

— Shoghi Effendi quoted in Compilations, *Lights of Guidance*, p. 473)

Also the Bible explains (Gen. 38:29 and Ruth 4:17) that Jesse is a descendant of Sarah.

The descendancy of Baha'u'llah from Sarah

The descendancy of Bahá'u'lláh from Sarah can also be explained historically, outside of the Bible.

Bahá'u'lláh belonged to the royal lineage of the Sasánian kings. It is to Yazdigird III, the last Sasásian king to occupy the throne of Iran, that the genealogy of Bahá'u'lláh can be traced. The first Sasánian king was Sasán who was the child of Cyrus the Persian who married a Jewish exile who belonged to the royal line of King David through Zerubbabel.

Zerubbabel was the governor of Judaea under the Persians. It is Zerubbabel who rebuilt the Temple (Encyclopedia Brittanica) according to a decree of Cyrus the Persian.

Cyrus is praised by Isaiah (Isaiah 45:1) as he granted permission to Jews to rebuild the temple.

"It is a tremendous and fascinating theme, Bahá'u'lláh's connection with the Faith of Judaism, and one which possesses great interest to Jew and Christian alike."

— Compilations, *Lights of Guidance*, p. 473

This is the time for the fulfilment of God's prophecies.

"Come ye blessed of my Father, inherit the Kingdom prepared for you from the foundation of the world"

— Matt. 25:34

Bahá'u'lláh, the Branch coming out of the roots of Jesse

Jesse is the father of King David. Isaiah foretold that a Branch will grow out of its roots. According to Isaiah, this Branch will be a Prophet. The coming of this Branch is very important as Isaiah links the coming of the Branch out of Jesse with the establishment of world peace.

" And there shall come forth a rod out of the stem of Jesse, and a Branch shall grow out of his roots: and the spirit of the LORD shall rest upon him, the spirit of wisdom and understanding, the spirit of counsel and might, the spirit of knowledge and of the fear of the LORD ...

The wolf also shall dwell with the lamb, and the leopard shall lie down with the kid; and the calf and the young ...They shall not hurt nor destroy in all my holy mountain: for the earth shall be full of the knowledge of the LORD, as the waters cover the sea.

— Isaiah 11:1-10

'Abdu'l-Bahá explains that Bahá'u'lláh is indeed the branch coming out of the roots of Jesse as above,

> *"conditions did not prevail in the time of the manifestation of Christ ... In the same way, universal peace did not come into existence in the time of Christ — that is to say, between the antagonistic and hostile nations there was neither peace nor concord, disputes and disagreements did not cease, and reconciliation and sincerity did not appear ...*
>
> *But these verses apply word for word to Bahá'u'lláh. Likewise in this marvellous cycle the earth will be transformed, and the world of humanity arrayed in tranquillity and beauty. Disputes, quarrels and murders will be replaced by peace, truth and concord; among the nations, peoples, races and countries, love and amity will appear. Cooperation and union will be established, and finally war will be entirely suppressed... Universal peace will raise its tent in the centre of the earth, and the blessed Tree of Life will grow and spread to such an extent that it will overshadow the East and the West. Strong and weak, rich and poor, antagonistic sects and hostile nations — which are like the wolf and the lamb, the leopard and kid, the lion and the calf — will act toward each other with the most complete love, friendship, justice and equity. The world will be filled with science, with the knowledge of the reality of the mysteries of beings, and with the knowledge of God"*

— Abdu'l-Bahá: *Some Answered Questions*, p. 62

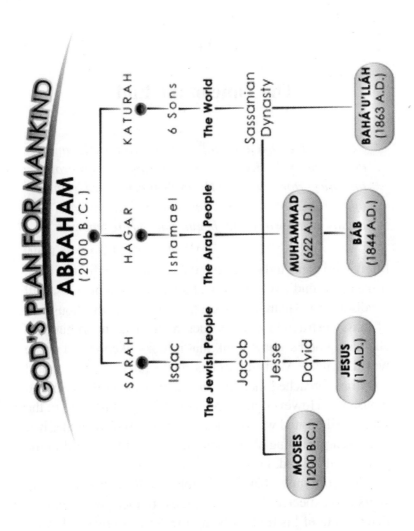

GOD'S PLAN FOR MANKIND
Three wives of Abraham

11

The Time of the End

"Each of the Divine Manifestations has a cycle, and during the cycle His laws and commandments prevail and are performed.When His cycle is completed by the appearance of the new Manifestation, a new cycle begins. In this way cycles begin, end and are renewed."

— 'Abdu'l-Bahá: *Some Answered Questions*, p. 160

Many Christians today believe that we are now living in the 'time of the end'. When people look around them and see all the disunity and hatred amongst the nations and the thousands of mass destruction devices such as nuclear, microbial and chemical bombs, some think that it looks like the end of the world is near. Many churches, especially in third world countries, preached that "the end will come in the year two thousand". However, the Bible never told us this was so; the year two thousand was never mentioned. Some churches had also been preaching about imminent end of the world in the year one thousand, but nothing happened.

Did you know that the disciples of Jesus two thousand years ago expected the 'end of times' in their own lifetime? Peter wrote of his time as being the *'end of times'*. (1 Peter 1:20, RVS, Revised Standard Version).

Was Peter wrong when he called the time of Jesus as 'the end of times"? No. The end of times has a spiritual meaning. This spiritual meaning in religion can be understood using the example of the sunrise and sunset. The sun sets on the old religion and rises on the new. The sun set on Moses at the end of His time and the new sun rose with the coming of Jesus. One follows the other.

Bible scholars pointed out that our commonly used translation of 'the end of times' is wrong. If we look in a few versions of the Bible we see:

- King James Version (published in AD 1611): *"The end of the world"*

- Revised Standard Version (published in AD 1951): *"The close of the age"*

- New International Version (published in AD 1978): *"End of the age"*

Bibles in simple English often use the expressions *'the last days'* or *'end of the world.'*[14] This causes some simple people to be really afraid of the literal imminent destruction of the world.

The phrase 'the time of the end' has been the cause of a lot of division amongst Christians because of the different interpretations that people have about its meaning and how and when it will be fulfilled.

We all know that Jesus did not write anything during his own lifetime. Jesus spoke a local language called Aramaic. The original words of Jesus came to us via several translations from one language into another.

Translation is a very difficult task and it is never perfect. The original Gospels were written in Greek, they were later translated into Latin and then into English. We now know from the Greek translations that Jesus never used the words the 'end of the world' or 'time of the end'. In the Greek text, the word 'aion' is used. This word means 'an era', 'a period of time' or 'an age'. If Jesus had really meant 'the end of the world, then we would have found the Greek word 'cosmos' used in the text. To correct this error in old translations modern bibles often use the phrase 'close of the age' instead.

'Close of the age'

What is 'an age' or 'an era'? The Oxford dictionary explains an age or an era as a period of time—for example, the length of time a person has existed or a very long time such as the Middle-Ages, or the Stone-Age. An era is a period in history that is noted for particular characteristics, for example the Buddhist era, the Christian era and now the Bahá'í era.

The 'close of the age' is not final but is followed by another period of time. When you grow up to be an adult you pass through different periods. First, you are a child. You only understand what it is to be a child. However, when you reach maturity the door of childhood is closed and a new door of understanding is opened. The age of childhood is closed and the age of adulthood is opened.

> *"When I was a child, I spoke as a child, I understood as a child, I thought as a child; but when I became a man, I put away childish things."*

— 1 Corinthians 13:11

Similarly, the whole of humanity has passed through different ages. The time of mankind's childhood is nearly over. Humanity is presently passing through an age of adolescence and is beginning to enter the age of maturity. Mankind is growing up. We are slowly leaving an old era of successive wars and rebellions and we are now struggling to enter a new era of peace. Once we enter maturity our problems won't cease but we will have the maturity to face the difficulties more easily and to overcome them. There are emerging international institutions that will be given greater powers to deal with the problems that humanity as a whole faces.

The banana plant can be used as an example of how what appears to be the end can in fact become the beginning of something new. As a banana stem matures, it produces a beautiful cluster of flowers that finally develop into the fruit. When we cut the fruit off the stem it rots. To an onlooker who is unaware of the potential for new growth it appears to be the end of the plant. But in fact it is the beginning of a new life. New shoots (suckers) appear from the root that will grow up into new stems to produce new fruit.

The close of an age is an eventful period

The end of one era and the beginning of a new era is a period full of problems and changes. It is very difficult for people to accept change. Let us reflect on the events of nearly two thousand years ago. After a long reign of power the Roman civilization with its false gods and corrupt lifestyle eventually collapsed. At the same time the Christian civilization which took more than three hundred years to establish rose up. During this transition period many of the early Christians were martyred. Such evil deeds demonstrate the extent to which people in power will go to stop change from happening.

A great historian Arnold Toynbee sees the history of humanity as the rise and fall of civilizations. He shows in his writings how every founder of a world religion has also been a founder of a civilization. The Christian civilization was based on the teachings of Jesus Christ. The Islamic civilization was built on the teachings of Muhammad. The Jewish culture that produced great kings such as Solomon and David arose on the laws and teachings of Moses. It was Zoroaster who provided the spiritual force that created the Persian Empire. The teachings of Krishna and Buddha as well as raising up great civilizations united millions of people in Asia under common codes of morals and behaviour. All those civilizations had their own works of art, architecture, great culture and heritage. Although this process affected various parts of the world in different ways and at different times it all helped to culturally shape our present day world.

There are two processes at work in the decline of an old and the birth of a new civilization – disintegration and integration. The disintegration is destroying and breaking down the old whilst integration is creating a new civilization. During this time world shaking and shaping events occur. There are usually wars which are part of the disintegration – a cleansing of age old prejudices and disunity. Then there are the forces of new ideals and goals that are released by the coming of the new Messenger of God with His new teachings. This provides the power that is needed to build unity in a new world.

When Jesus arose this signalled the end of the Roman civilization. It did not happen immediately and it was not really the end of everything. Gradually a new civilization was born based on His teachings – the Western Christian civilization. Thus, the end of an era means the end of a civilization that is based on outworn institutions and ideas and the beginning of a new civilization based on the renewal of the eternal Teachings of God.

Today we are living at the beginning of a new era

There are more than fifteen prophecies relating to the year AD 1844 as the beginning of a new era. The reason that we still have many problems today is because mankind has not yet accepted the Teachings and Laws of Bahá'u'lláh, the new Messenger of God for this age. Bahá'u'lláh can be likened to a skilled physician who sees the patient, diagnoses the illness then prescribes the remedy. If the patient refuses to take the medicine prescribed then he will not be cured. Is that the fault of the doctor? Absolutely not, He has done his duty. So it also is with the world. Only a Divine Physician can see the entire complexity of problems facing the world. However, if the patient (humanity) refuses to take the remedy (the new Teachings from God) then the civilization will become sicker and sicker as we see today.

"The All-Knowing Physician hath His finger on the pulse of mankind. He perceiveth the disease, and prescribeth, in His unerring wisdom, the remedy."

— Bahá'u'lláh: *Gleanings from the Writings of Bahá'u'lláh*, p. 212

"Its sickness [the world] is approaching the stage of utter hopelessness, inasmuch as the true Physician is debarred from administering the remedy, whilst unskilled practitioners are regarded with favor, and are accorded full freedom to act."

— Bahá'u'lláh: *Gleanings from the Writings of Bahá'u'lláh*, p. 39

What will be the fate of humanity if it refuses to accept the teachings of Bahá'u'lláh?

Never before in human history has mankind come so close to world consciousness. Thanks to the tremendous technical progress in transport and communication systems. Mankind has learned to fly through the sky like the birds and swim through the sea like the fishes. When the astronauts travelled to the moon and looked back at the earth they gained a new realisation of this planet as our home. Mankind is one family, the family of man, living together in our home. How is it possible then for the members of one family living together to remain divided? How is it possible that some are overburdened with riches whilst others are living and suffering in enormous poverty? Would this be possible in one family where all the members loved one another and helped each other?

Bahá'u'lláh lived at a time when people travelled on horses and donkeys. He foretold with an infallible foresight how to establish world unity. The social evolution of humanity has brought us from the level of the caveman to the tribe, to the village, to the city state, then to nationhood. The next step, in the words of a great Christian thinker, Teilhard de Chardin, is the "planetization of mankind".

The Universal House of Justice wrote in the statement "The Promise of World Peace" addressed to the peoples of the world:

> *"Whether peace is to be reached only after unimaginable horror precipitated by humanity's stubborn clinging to old patterns of behaviour, or is to be embraced now by an act of consultative will, is the choice before all who inhabit the earth."*
>
> — The Universal House of Justice: *The Promise of World Peace*, p. 1

It is not God, as many people think, who will come down to earth to punish the people for not listening to Him. It is humanity who will punish itself. God cannot be blamed for mankind's actions that are taken with our own free will.

The following statement was by 'Abdu'l-Bahá:

> *"There is in existence a stupendous force, as yet, happily undiscovered by man. Let us supplicate God ... that this force be not discovered by science until spiritual civilization shall dominate the human mind. In the hands of men of lower nature, this power would be able to destroy the whole earth.*
>
> — 'Abdu'l-Bahá quoted by Shoghi Effendi: *Japan Will Turn Ablaze*, p. 51

Was it coincidence or a warning that those words were used by 'Abdu'l-Bahá in 1912 when He spoke to the ambassador of Japan? It was Japan that would experience thirty-four years later the horror of nuclear power with the destruction of two cities, Hiroshima and Nagasaki, causing the death of more than two hundred thousand people in less than a minute.

God will never destroy the world

In several passages, both in the Old and New Testaments, the Bible mentions that the world will pass through fiery tribulations such as it has never before seen, but that God's Kingdom will be established on earth as a result of these difficult times:

> "And I saw a new heaven and a new earth: for the first heaven and the first earth were passed away; and there was no more sea."
>
> (Revelation 21:1)

All these word images - first heaven, first earth, new heaven, new earth explain that the world, through dire calamities, will be chastened and purified, and hence prepared for the new civilization in which there will be no borders between countries (no more sea) or in the words of Bahá'u'lláh:

> "It is not for him to pride himself who loveth his own country, but rather for him who loveth the whole world. The earth is but one country and mankind its citizens."
>
> — Gleanings from the Writings of Bahá'u'lláh, p. 250

There are many other verses in the Bible which lead us to the understanding that no matter how much the world suffers in the end-time tribulations there is a better world waiting on the other side of these dark days.

Indeed, many terrible things occur at the end of an era. They can be so bad that many people will think that this is the end of the world. We are promised in the Bible that the entire world will not be destroyed as God will show mercy and shorten those terrible days.

"And if those days had not been shortened, no human being would be saved: but for the sake of the elect, those days will be shortened."

— Matt. 24:22

Also in the Old Testament we find the following promise. We all know the story about the Arc of Noah and the flood. God made a solemn promise never to do this again.

"Neither will I ever destroy every living creature as I have done ..."

— Genesis 8:21

To remind us of this promise, the story continues, God sets up a rainbow in the sky as a sign of this agreement.

"I have set my rainbow in the cloud, and it will be the sign of the covenant between me and the earth."

— Genesis 9:13

Whenever we see the beautiful multi-coloured rainbow appear in the darkened sky, we know that the bright sun will soon shine again. God has also promised us through His Messengers that after the darkness of war and hatred we will again see the sunshine of love and unity in the world. The birth of a new era is like the birth of a child. This process is very painful, but afterwards the joy helps us to forget the suffering.

12

The Kingdom of God

"Unto what is the Kingdom of God like? and whereunto shall I resemble it? It is like a grain of mustard seed, which a man took, and cast into his garden; and it grew, and waxed a great tree ..."

— Luke 13:18–19

The Kingdom of God is within you

In the New Testament, John the Baptist was preaching, *"Repent ye, for the kingdom of heaven is at hand."* (Matt. 3:2) When Jewish priests asked Jesus when the Kingdom of God would come, Jesus answered;

"... behold, the Kingdom of God is within you."

— Luke 17:21

Here Jesus told the Jewish priests that only when God is the King and ruler of our hearts can we enter the Kingdom of God. *"Blessed are the pure in heart: for they shall see God."* (Matt. 5:8) How can we develop this pure heart so that we can enter into the Kingdom of God? The answer is to love God.

"Thou shalt love the Lord Thy God with all thy heart, and with all thy soul, and with all thy mind. This is the first and great commandment."

— Matt. 22:37–38

The Kingdom and the Will of God

Jesus says, *"Not everyone who says to me 'Lord, Lord' shall enter the kingdom of heaven, but he who does the will of my Father in heaven."* (Matt. 7:21) His words show that it is important to discover the will of God. It is not sufficient to say 'I believe' or to cry out 'Lord, Lord'; this alone will not get you into heaven. Anyone who wants to enter the Kingdom of God must seek to follow the will of God.

He made it clear that the will of God will prevail on earth in the 'Lord's Prayer' in which He asks his disciples to pray *"Thy Kingdom come, Thy will be done on earth as it is in heaven."* These words of Jesus are both a prayer and a prophecy.

The Kingdom of God established on earth

Jesus says that the Kingdom of God is within you. Then the Lord's Prayer says that the Kingdom of God will be established when the people follow the will of God on earth as it is in heaven. The disciples were very familiar with the coming of the Kingdom. Its coming was associated with certain signs and prophecies that must be fulfilled. The Bible promised a time when there is peace throughout the world. (Isaiah 2:4, Micah 4:4–5, Isaiah 15:1–2 and Joel 3:18).

A time of justice:

"Righteousness and peace have kissed each other."

— Psalm 85:10

Many Christians are very impatiently waiting for the coming of the Kingdom of God. They often think that the Kingdom of God is a great city that will suddenly appear descending out of heaven.

"...and showed me that great city, the holy Jerusalem descending out of heaven from God having the glory of God..."

— John 21, 10:11

Jesus explains to us that the Kingdom of God will not instantly appear and suddenly descend but rather will appear gradually. He compares the Kingdom of God with a seed that takes time to grow and rise up.

"Unto what is the Kingdom of God like? and where unto shall I resemble it? It is like a grain of mustard seed, which a man took, and cast into his garden; and it grew, and waxed a great tree ..."

— Luke 13:18–19[15]

In comparison to a tree, a mustard seed is very small. This idea of the gradual rising up of the Kingdom of God is repeated in another example:

"And again he said, Whereunto shall I liken the kingdom of God? It is like leaven ..."

— Luke 13:20–1

When you make bread, only a little yeast is used with a lot of flour. However, the yeast hidden inside the flour causes the dough to gradually rise. Hence, the idea that the Kingdom of God will appear gradually comes from Jesus' own teachings.

It also is affirmed by Shoghi Effendi, the Guardian of the Bahá'í Faith when he tells us that the Kingdom of God which already exists in the spiritual worlds will appear in this world by degrees as mankind conforms itself to those spiritual teachings and principles brought by Bahá'u'lláh.

Bahá'ís throughout the world are engaged in building this Kingdom on earth by their actions in the community. They are reaching out and offering their neighbours and friends core activities which include sharing the Word of God in study circles, offering neighbourhood children's classes and junior youth classes as well as devotional meetings to meditate and pray together. This is all done in a spirit of service which Bahá'u'lláh says is equal to worship. In this age morality is active not passive

– the world is tired of just words and requires to see deeds of purity. The Bahá'í Faith is offering a model or a framework of action that will bring the Kingdom of God on earth.

The world is now physically ready

In the time of Jesus, Jews had a very limited understanding of the extent of the world. They did not know that Australia, China or America existed. Jesus could not have explained about the oneness of mankind because they did not know that other groups of people, such as the Aborigines, Chinese or American Indians existed. Referring to their limited understanding Jesus said:

> *"I have yet many things to say unto you, but ye cannot bear them now."*
>
> — John 16:12–13

Bahá'u'lláh's Revelation released the Holy Spirit which gave the world a fresh spiritual impulse to create all the changes in technology, development and human rights for mankind to come of age. One of His teachings is the harmony of science and religion. It is vital for mankind's progress and protection that the world develops equally and at the same time in the fields of science as well as in spiritual maturity. If the love of God is in man's heart he will use his wonderful inventions to benefit mankind rather than destroy it. Bahá'u'lláh foretold with an infallible foresight how to establish the oneness of mankind which will lead to the establishment of the Kingdom of God on earth. Thanks to modern inventions such as airplanes, television, satellites and computers the world has become more like one country with mankind its citizens. It is only after the coming of Bahá'u'lláh that humanity has reached the point of development in international travel and communication to physically establish the Christ-promised Kingdom of God on earth.

Developments on the Mountain of God

Bahá'u'lláh announced in His Tablet of Carmel:

*"Rejoice, for God hath in this day established upon thee
His throne, hath made thee the dawning-place of His signs
and the dayspring of the evidences of His Revelation."*

The Bahá'í world centre is in Israel. It is built on Mt. Carmel.
Any visitor to Haifa in Israel can witness how an entire mountain
has been transformed into the complex of majestic buildings
spread out along the Arc and the flights of terraced gardens rising
from the foot of the mountain to its summit. It is a visible sign
that the Cause of Bahá'u'lláh's influence has steadily expanded
throughout the world. The crowds of visitors from every land
throng the stairs and pathways each day and a stream of
distinguished guests are welcomed to the World Centre. Perceptive
minds already sense the dawning fulfilment of the vision recorded
twenty-three hundred years ago by the prophet Isaiah.

This vision tells us about Mt. Carmel (which means the
Mountain of the Lord). He tells us that it is from this mountain
that the law will go forth and peace will be established:

*"And it shall come to pass in the last days, that the
mountain of the LORD's house shall be established
in the top of the mountains, and shall be exalted above
the hills; and all nations shall flow unto it.*

*And many people shall go and say, Come ye, and let us
go up to the mountain of the LORD, to the house of the
God of Jacob; and he will teach us of his ways, and we
will walk in his paths: for out of Zion shall go forth the
law, and the word of the LORD from Jerusalem.*

*And he shall judge among the nations, and shall
rebuke many people: and they shall beat their swords
into ploughshares, and their spears into pruning*

hooks: nation shall not lift up sword against nation,
neither shall they learn war any more."

— Isaiah 2:2-4

It is to this mountain that all nations flow when Bahá'ís of the world go to visit the Bahá'í Holy places and elect the Universal House of Justice. *"The excellency of Carmel and Sharon, they shall see the glory of the Lord ..."* (Isaiah 35:2) The Glory of the Lord is the translation of Bahá'u'lláh's name from Arabic into English.

The Universal House of Justice which is the international body of the worldwide Bahá'í community is now firmly established on the Mountain of God where it co-ordinates the worldwide activities of Bahá'ís and is a source of guidance for mankind. All these prophecies were fulfilled through the coming of Bahá'u'lláh to the Holy Land, not by His own wish, but by banishment as a prisoner. He was sent there in exile from His own country.

The Arc of Salvation

The Old Testament tells us that God commanded Noah to build an Arc to save mankind. It was part of God's plan for that time. The buildings of the World Centre which include the seat of the Universal House of Justice are spread out in the shape of an Arc. Bahá'u'lláh says: *"Call out to Zion, O Carmel...Ere long will God sail His Arc upon thee and will manifest the people of Bahá who have been mentioned in the Book of Names"*. This is the new Arc of salvation for today which is part of the plan of God for making the Kingdom of God on earth a reality as mentioned in the Lord's Prayer.

"Thy kingdom come, Thy will be done in earth, as it
is in heaven."

— Matthew 6:10

Appendix

Invitation to join the Bahá'í Faith

An important principle of the Bahá'í Faith is the independent investigation of Truth. Therefore it is between you and your Creator whether you wish to become a follower of Bahá'u'lláh. The Bahá'í Faith has no priests or clergy. It also has no sacraments or rituals such as baptism.

The process of becoming a Bahá'í is very simple. Once you feel in your heart that Bahá'u'lláh is the latest Messenger from God you can fill in a registration card which is available from any member or institution of the Bahá'í community where you reside. You can find a local telephone listing for the Bahá'í Local Spiritual Assembly or the National Spiritual Assembly in your area. The registration card will have the following declaration:

"I wish to become a member of the Bahá'í community. I accept Bahá'u'lláh as the Bearer of God's message for this Day and will endeavour to follow His teachings and the Bahá'í way of life. I also accept the authority of the institutions which administer the affairs of the Bahá'í community."

Bibliography

K. Latourette: *A History of Christianity*, Harper and Row, New York, 1953.

The New Encyclopaedia Britannica, University of Chicago, USA, 15th ed., 1990.

D. E. Barrett: *World Christian Encyclopaedia*, Oxford University Press, 1982.

J. M. Munck: *The Acts of the Apostles*, The Anchor Bible, New York, 1985.

John Shelby Spong : *Rescuing the Bible from fundamentalism, A bishop rethinks the meaning of scripture*, Harper, San Francisco, 1992.

John Shelby Spong : *Why Christianity must change or die*, Harper, San Francisco, 1998.

Paul Johnson: *A History of Christianity*, Penguin Books, Great Britain, 1979.

Daniel J. Grolin: *Jesus, and early Christianity in the Gospels,* George Ronald Oxford, 2002.

J. E. Esslemont: *Bahá'u'lláh and the New Era,* Bahá'í Publishing Trust, India.

Balyuzi: *'Abdu'l-Bahá, the Centre of the Covenant*, George Ronald, London, Great Britain, 1971.

H. Hornby: *Lights of Guidance*, Bahá'í Publishing Trust, New Delhi, 1983.

Gary L. Matthews: *He Cometh with Clouds,* George Ronald, Great Britain, 1996. (www.stonehaven-press.com)

William Sears: *The Wine of Astonishment*, George Ronald, Great Britain, 1985.

William Sears: *The Prince of Peace*, Bahá'í Publishing Trust, India, 1986, rp 2005.

William Sears: *Thief in the Night*, George Ronald, Great Britain, 1981.

William Sears: *The Wine of Astonishment*, George Ronald, 1985.

Gayle Woolson: *Divine Symphony*, Bahá'í Publishing Trust, India, 1977.

Michael Sours: *A Study of Baha'u'llah's Tablet to the Christians*, One World Publications, 1990.

George Townshend: *Christ and Bahá'u'lláh*, George Ronald, Oxford, 1957.

Hushidar Motlagh: *I Shall Come Again*, Global Perspective, 1992. (www.globalperspective.org)

The Light of Bahá'u'lláh, National Spiritual Assembly of the Bahá'ís of the United States, Bahá'í Publishing Trust, USA, 1982. (www.bahai.org)

Holy Writings

The Holy Bible, King James Version, American Bible Society, 1972.

The New International Study Bible, Michigan, USA,1985.

Bahá'u'lláh: *Gleanings of the Writings of Bahá'u'lláh*, Bahá'í Publishing Trust, Wilmette, Illinois. 1976.

Bahá'u'lláh: *The Book of Certitude,* Bahá'í Publishing Trust, 1931.

Bahá'u'lláh: *The Hidden Words*, Bahá'í Publishing Trust, USA, 1974.

Bahá'u'lláh: *The Seven Valleys*, Bahá'í Publishing Trust, USA, 1974.

Bahá'u'lláh: *The Proclamation of Bahá'u'lláh*, Bahá'í World Centre, Israel, 1972.

'Abdu'l-Bahá: *Foundations of World Unity*, Bahá'í Publishing Trust, Wilmette, Illinois, USA, 1945.

'Abdu'l-Bahá: *Paris Talks*, London: Bahá'í Publishing Trust, 1953, rp 1976.

'Abdu'l-Bahá: *Selections from the Writings of 'Abdu'l-Bahá*, Bahá'í World Centre, 1978.

'Abdu'l-Bahá: *Some Answered Questions*, Bahá'í Publishing Trust, USA, 1981.

'Abdu'l-Bahá: *The Secret of Divine Civilization*, Bahá'í Publishing Trust, Wilmette, Illinois. 1970.

Shoghi Effendi: *The World Order of Bahá'u'lláh*, Bahá'í Publishing Trust, Wilmette, Illinois. 1938.

Notes and References

1   NIV is an abbreviation for the New International Version of the Bible.

2   This "cleaning of the Temple" comes after a 2,300 day period of "desolation" during which it is corrupted by sinful misbehaviour from the Jews. The greatest sin committed by Jews was not to listen to God's word. "The abomination of desolation" meant they were not able to worship in their Temple as it was used for worship of pagan Gods by their enemies and they were forced to leave Israel and live in exile. Only in 1844 were they allowed to return back to Israel. This would gradually lead to the restoration of the temple rights of the Jews.

3   Some Christians still believe that in 1844 a spiritual event took place in heaven! For example, the Seventh-Day Adventists (formally created in 1963) believe that their founder Mrs White is a prophet. Mrs White wrote that in the summer of 1844 Jesus entered into the most holy place of the heavenly sanctuary to perform the closing work of atonement preparatory to His coming. (White E. G.: The Triumph of God's Love, p. 252) SDA regards Mrs White writings as a continuing and authoritive source of truth and they continue to proclaim that Christ will return soon.

4   'The anointed one' was a title given to kings as in a ceremony, some oil was poured on their head as a symbol for their appointment as king (see Volume2).

5   Some Bibles use the term 'tribulation' instead of its actual Greek meaning 'oppression'. Both mean the same: a time of spiritual confusion and destruction. The most important is

the 'spiritual confusion' as it is a greater calamity for the eternal soul to be lost by confusion than for temporary bodies to be destroyed.

6   "Woe unto you, scribes and Pharisees, hypocrites! for ye are as graves" (Luke 11:44) and "Ye serpents, ye generation of vipers, how can ye escape the damnation of hell?" (Matt. 23:33)

7   The Bahá'í writings tell us that every word in the Holy Writings has several meanings. For example, Bahá'u'lláh gives several meanings to the allusion of clouds: *"those things that are contrary to the ways and desires of all men. ...* [such as] *the annulment of laws, the abrogation of former Dispensations, the repeal of rituals and customs current amongst men, the exalting of the illiterate faithful above the learned opposers of the Faith. In another sense, they mean the appearance of the* [Promised One] *... in the image of mortal man, with such human limitations as eating and drinking, poverty and riches, glory and abasement, sleeping and waking, and such other things as cast doubt in the minds of men ..."* (Bahá'u'lláh: *The Kitáb-i-Íqán (The Book of Certitude),* pp. 71–2.)

8   As we will explain later, the spirit of Bahá'u'lláh came from heaven but His body came from the womb of His mother. As with Jesus, Bahá'u'lláh did not attend any school, but by the time He was 12 years old, He was able to explain the most difficult parts of the Holy Writings. This kind of knowledge, which is a direct gift of God, is called innate knowledge.

9   Trumpets are also used to announce the approach of a King or the proclamation of an important announcement. The trumpet symbolizes Bahá'u'lláh's revelation that calls people to God and announces the Glad Tidings of God's word amongst humankind.

10   Imagine that Christ really returned descending on a cloud in the visible sky. Then everyone would have no choice but to believe. Hence, there would be no freedom, no love, and it

would not be possible to pass judgement on anyone. All humans would behave like perfect robots forever!

11   "Bahá'u'lláh declared that religion is in complete harmony with science and reason." ('Abdu'l-Bahá: *The Promulgation of Universal Peace*, p. 231)

12   During the Crusades, Christian Europe was living in the 'dark ages'. Europeans were very primitive. At the same time, in Asia, Islam had given birth to a great new civilization. There was peace. The Christian Crusaders were very surprised when they arrived in the Muslim cities around the year 1200. The Moslem cities were full of light and were well organized. In Europe, it was not safe to travel on the roads as there were many robbers, but in the East people could travel freely during the day and the night without being afraid of being robbed. A peaceful society allowed the arts, literature and sciences to become highly developed. Thanks to Islam and the Islamic knowledge that the warriors brought back from the East, Christian Europe left 'the dark ages' and a new civilization, called "the Renaissance" was born.

13   The year 1844 is the time of renewal of the religion of God and refers to the beginning of the Bahá'í Faith. The Báb declared His Mission in 1844. This was called "the second woe" by St. John. Why associate the coming of a new Messenger of God with a woe or a warning? Because in the beginning the coming of the Messenger of God brings with it a lot of woe or sorrow, grief and distress. First, there is the suffering of the Messenger of God Himself, and then of his followers who are martyred for His sake. In the Bible, the Advent of Jesus was also called the dreadful day of the Lord. (Malachi 4:5) It is also the time of judgement between the lovers of God who accept His new Messenger, and the unbelievers who reject Him. Woe to them who reject Him, theirs is the greatest loss. John spoke of three woes or warnings. The first woe or warning was Muhammad.

(Rev. 9:12) The second woe was the Báb. The third woe, which came quickly thereafter, was Bahá'u'lláh, even as John prophesied: *"The second woe is past; and, behold the third woe cometh quickly."* There was only a brief period of 19 years between the declaration of the Báb and the declaration of Bahá'u'lláh.

14 Bahá'u'lláh issued a similar warning: *"Beware that thou allow not the wolf to become the shepherd of God's flock ..."* (Gleanings from the Writings of Bahá'u'lláh, p. 233.)

15 The mound of ancient Shushan is adjacent to the village of <u>Shúsh, 380 km ESE of Baghdád.</u>

16 Micah foretold the place of birth of Jesus. *"Out of Bethlehem, a ruler of Israel* will arise." (Micah 5:2) Bethlehem is also the birthplace of King David.

17 The early followers of Jesus came from a Jewish tradition where it is forbidden to make images. Most pictures that we see of 'Jesus' have European features. Since they are a product of the imagination of painters, they can <u>not show</u> the true physical form of Jesus. He was rarely portrayed as a Jew during the Middle Ages and the Renaissance. At that time, Jews were despised and persecuted in Western Europe. They were often blamed and held responsible for the death of Jesus on the cross.

18 Bahá'u'lláh quoted in H. M. Balyuzi: (*Bahá'u'lláh: The King of Glory*, p. 78)

19 More than 30 prophecies can be found in Baha'u'llah's Writings. They are detailed and specific, often mentioning the names and the location of the future event. Most of those prophecies were widely distributed and often ridiculed because people thought them impossible. Who would expect that powerful kingdoms would suddenly disappear, that powerful rulers would end up as prisoners, or that powerful religious leaders would loose their power and domination over

the people? However, everything happened exactly as Bahá'u'lláh had foretold. Bahá'u'lláh invites all seekers to study these prophecies. He wrote that amongst "the clearest proofs" that "attest the truth of His Cause" is the fact that all His prophecies have been fulfilled. Since a detailed study of those prophesies is beyond the scope of this book, we invite you to read *He cometh with clouds* by Gary L. Matthews.

20 Israel did not exist then. The country was called Palestine and at that time was part of the Ottoman Empire (Turkey).

21 For the first time in world history, we posses the original writings of a Prophet of God, signed by that Prophet Himself. These writings are kept on Mt. Carmel, in Israel. Many of these writings are in Arabic. It normally takes many years of disciplined instruction to be able to write well in Arabic. *"Bahá'u'lláh had never studied Arabic; He had not had a tutor or teacher, nor had He entered a school. Nevertheless, the eloquence and elegance of His blessed expositions in Arabic, as well as His Arabic writings, caused astonishment and stupefaction to the most accomplished Arabic scholars, and all recognized and declared that He was incomparable and unequalled."* ('Abdu'l-Bahá: *Some Answered Questions*, p. 34)

22 Adapted from Adib Taherzadeh: (*The Covenant of Bahá'u'lláh*)

23 The marriage of Cyrus had great consequences as it would lead to the rebuilding of the Temple in Jerusalem! "And Cyrus took to wife the daughter of Salathiel, the sister of Zerubbabel, and he took her to wife according to the law of the Persians, and made her [his] queen. And she entreated Cyrus to bring about the return of the children of Israel [to Jerusalem]. And inasmuch as Zerubbabel was her brother, she was very insistent about the return to Jerusalem of those who had been led away into captivity. Now Cyrus loved his wife as he loved himself, and he did for her what she wished. ...Cyrus said

unto Zerubbabel, his wife's brother, "Rise up, and take with thee all the children of thy people, and go up to Jerusalem in peace; and [re]build the city of thy fathers, and dwell and reign therein. And because Cyrus brought about the return of the children of Israel [to Jerusalem], God said, "I have taken my servant Cyrus by his right hand" (Isaiah 44:25) (Extracted from the "Syriac Cave of Treasures" p.168)

24 There are several missionary organizations that specialize in the translation of the Bible into tribal languages. They often strike terror in the hearts of the simple villagers when they translate *"The end of the world"*. Many villagers, believing that these words are the words of God, are expecting the end of the world to come soon. They even stop working, and wait for Jesus to come back on the cloud.

25 This allegory causes great problems for those comparing the description with the properties of common mustard plants (black or white/yellow). These are annual herbs with small seeds that grow to a height of 1 to 3.7 m (black). This story may more reasonably refer to the "toothbrush tree" (*Salvadora persica*) or Khardal (this is the word used in Arabic Bibles) that grows in Galilee. It has small (1 to 4 mm diameter) seeds, grows to a height of 2 to 4 m, and has the flavour and properties of mustard.